WEEKEND MAKES

SIMPLE APPLIQUÉ

25 QUICK AND EASY PROJECTS TO MAKE

WEEKEND MAKES

SIMPLE APPLIQUÉ

25 QUICK AND EASY PROJECTS TO MAKE

JANET GODDARD

First published 2019 by
Guild of Master Craftsman Publications Ltd Castle Place,
166 High Street, Lewes,
East Sussex, BN7 1XU

Senior Project Editor: Beth Dymond
Managing Art Editor: Darren Brant
Art Editor: Laura Hurst
Photographer: Jesse Wild
Stylists: Jaine Bevan & Jenny Howard

Colour origination by GMC Reprographics
Printed and bound in China

CONTENTS

INTRODUCTION

Welcome to **Weekend Makes – Simple Appliqué**; a book featuring twenty-five fresh, bright and modern projects to make for yourself, your home or to give as gifts.

Life can be busy, and we don't always have the time to be able to commit to larger or more difficult projects, which can be just too time-consuming. However, each of the appliquéd projects in this book can easily be completed in a weekend. Some are super quick and can be stitched in just an hour, while others will take a few hours or a day. The projects are graded as 'Easy' or 'Requires Experience'. Basic sewing skills are needed for the 'Easy' projects, which are suitable for beginners. The 'Requires Experience' projects have a few more steps and will take a little longer to make.

Appliqué is one of the oldest forms of needlework and simply means applying one piece of fabric on top of another to create a picture or motif. A motif appliquéd to a project embellishes the item and gives it a personalized look. There is a range of projects in this book including bags, purses, tableware, sewing items, pencil cases and more, and each item is appliquéd with one or more simple motifs to bring it to life.

A section on appliqué techniques can be found at the front of the book. This details the variety of methods that can be used to appliqué either on the sewing machine or by hand. If you are new to appliqué I suggest that you try out a number of methods and then choose your favourite to use. Any of the methods can be used to stitch any of the projects in this book. All of the motifs can be found at the back of the book and are drawn to size.

I love working with fabric and have enjoyed using a wide range of colours and prints to make these projects. The really great thing about appliqué is that you can raid your fabric stash for small pieces of fabric to create the motifs. Each pattern includes sewing instructions, step-by-step photos and finishing techniques, as well as a few tips.

The twenty-five projects in this book are stylish but also practical for everyday use. I have so enjoyed designing and making them and hope that you enjoy stitching them too.

Janet Goddard

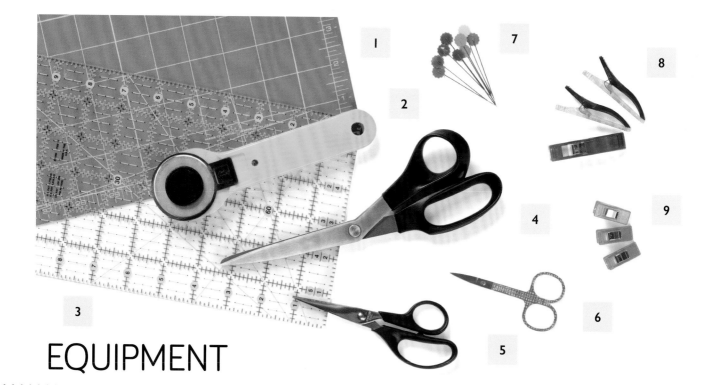

EQUIPMENT

Good-quality basic equipment is needed. There is no need to spend a fortune on the latest gadgets; just invest in some good-quality essential resources.

Sewing machine: The most important piece of equipment for stitching these Weekend Makes is a sewing machine. It really only needs to be able to stitch forwards and backwards and have a zigzag stitch; it doesn't need a whole lot of fancy stitches, although a blanket stitch can be used for some appliqué, if desired. It is important to care for your machine and to clean and service it regularly to keep it working well. A little oil, applied according to the manufacturer's instructions, should help to keep everything in good order. Changing the needle regularly also helps with the quality of stitching, so I usually change the needle on the machine every time I begin a new project. The machine feet used the most are the ¼in (0.65cm) patchwork foot, which is excellent for maintaining ¼in (0.65cm) wide seams; the open foot for zigzag, blanket stitch and straight stitch machine appliqué; the zipper foot for stitching in zips and the walking foot for machine quilting.

Rotary cutter, ruler and mat: All the fabric pieces for the construction of the projects ready to be appliquéd can be cut using a rotary cutting mat (**1**), a rotary cutter (**2**) and a ruler (**3**).

A rotary cutting mat is a self-healing mat designed to be used with a rotary cutter. Mats come with grid markings on them, which can be used with the ruler for accurate cutting. If you are purchasing a mat for the first time, buy the largest you can afford. A 24 × 36in (61 × 91cm) mat is a good investment.

A rotary cutter is a cutting instrument with a round-wheeled blade. This is used with an acrylic ruler and a self-healing cutting mat. A good-quality rotary cutter should have a protective safety shield on it that can be pushed on and off. It is important to train yourself to always make sure that the safety cover is on the blade every time the cutter is put down. Blades are sharp and can cut through up to eight layers of fabric at a time and so can do a lot of damage to hands if not kept safe. Replace the blades when they start to become blunt.

Rulers come in many shapes and sizes, are marked in inches or centimetres and are made of tough acrylic. I personally find the rulers with yellow markings the easiest to see on fabric, but this is a personal choice. If you are purchasing a single ruler, make it a 6 × 24in (15 × 61cm) one as this can be used for most projects.

Scissors: A good sharp pair of dressmaking scissors **(4)** is essential for tasks such as cutting through cotton wadding (batting). A medium-size pair **(5)** is useful for cutting off corners and trimming, while a small pair **(6)** is handy for snipping threads and for hand sewing.

Pins: I use flat flower head fine pins **(7)** when sewing, as they help to keep the fabric flat, but any type of pins will do.

Needles: Hand sewing needles are used for the hand appliqué and some finishing off techniques and are available in many sizes. Sharps are good for general sewing and hand stitching binding.

Clips: These are great for holding multiple layers together when hand stitching a binding or topstitching around the top of a project **(8** and **9)**. The clips are plastic (think mini clothes pegs but better) and can be removed easily as you stitch.

Fabric markers: There are many fabric markers **(10)** available, but any marker should be easy to use, clear to see and simple to remove after you have finished sewing. Markers are used to mark measurements for cutting or stitching and also quilting lines or patterns. Several different markers are needed in order to contrast with both light and dark fabrics. White and silver markers, water-erasable pens and chalk markers are all useful.

Seam ripper: This is often called a 'quick unpick' and usually comes as a tool with the sewing machine **(11)**. It is useful for removing tacking (basting) stitches or the odd mistake we all make now and then.

Safety pins: These are really useful for holding layers of fabric and wadding (batting) together when quilting **(12)**.

Thread: Thread to match the colour of the fabrics to be appliquéd is essential for both hand and machine appliqué, while black thread can be used for the straight stitch appliqué **(13)**. A selection of pale grey, dark grey and beige threads are the most useful colours for piecing.

Iron and ironing board: A press with a good-quality dry iron makes all the difference to a finished product. The ironing surface needs to be firm and clean.

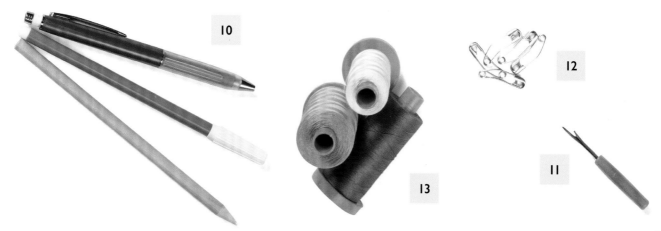

MEASUREMENTS AND TEMPLATES

All the cutting instructions for the projects include a ¼in (0.65cm) seam allowance. I have used imperial as the standard measurement throughout all my patterns, but the metric measurements have been included as well. Use either imperial or metric, and do not mix the two together.

All of the templates for the appliqué can be found at the back of the book and are printed at full size. They have all been reversed for transferring to the wrong side of the fabrics to be appliquéd.

FABRIC, FUSIBLES AND THREAD

One of the nicest parts of starting a new project is being able to choose the fabrics. I have made fabric choices to suit the project design. If the project uses large shapes I have tended to use fabric that has a larger-scale print design; for smaller shapes the fabric print has tended to be smaller as well.

All of the projects in this book use fabric that is 100 per cent cotton and of a high quality. Other natural fibres such as wool or silk can be used to great effect in appliqué; however, because they can shrink and fray, they should be pre-washed before use. The fabrics used in this book are bright, modern and there are a variety of patterns. Each project details the fabric colour and print used but you can substitute your own fabric choices to suit.

The fabric allowances in the patterns are for fabric that is approximately 42in (107cm) wide from selvedge to selvedge. I always cut the selvedge from the fabric before beginning a project and rarely pre-wash fabrics, but this is a personal choice.

The fabric allowances in each pattern allow for approximately 2–3in (5–7.5cm) extra, so if a small mistake is made you shouldn't run out of fabric. However, do try to be as careful as possible. Where the pattern has listed scraps in the materials list it is assumed that each scrap of fabric would be a 6in (15.2cm) square or less.

Fusible web is a heat-activated adhesive that allows you to use an iron to bond fabrics together. I have used a lightweight fusible web for all of the machine-stitched projects and also the blanket stitch hand appliquéd projects. Most varieties of fusible web are paper backed, which allows you to draw or trace your motifs onto the adhesive and then bond to the fabric.

I have used freezer paper for the needle turn hand appliquéd projects. Freezer paper is a waxy, shiny paper that sticks to the fabric when heated and then peels away cleanly on removal.

The best thread for appliqué is a high-quality cotton thread. I tend to use a 50-weight thread in a matching colour to the fabric for the appliqué and a grey thread for all the piecing. For quilting I use a 40-weight thread in a colour that complements or contrasts with the fabric.

ROTARY CUTTING

Most of the fabric pieces for the patterns in this book can be cut using a rotary cutter. If you are new to using a rotary cutter it is worth spending some time practising on scrap fabric, as accuracy does improve with practice.

To cut safely, always hold the cutter firmly in your hand at a 45-degree angle and place your other hand on the ruler. The hand on the ruler needs to be flat with the fingers slightly opened, making sure that your fingers are away from the edges of the ruler. Flip the safety cover off the cutter and place the blade next to the ruler. Starting at the bottom of the fabric, begin to cut away from yourself until you have cut past the end of the fabric (1).

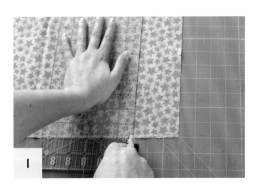

Close the safety cover on the cutter before putting the cutter down. It is easier to stand and cut rather than sit, and a kitchen work surface is usually at an appropriate height.

Before you make your first cut, iron the fabric to remove any wrinkles.

Fold the fabric selvedge to selvedge. If you use a 24in (61cm) long ruler you should not need to fold the fabric again, but if your ruler is shorter you may need to fold the fabric again so that the fold is on the selvedge. Ensure that all the layers are smooth. Place the ruler firmly on top of the fabric and cut the selvedge from the fabric, tidying up any uneven edges (2).

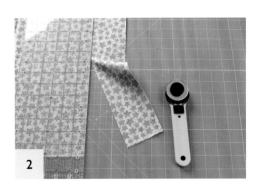

To cut strips of fabric from which further shapes can be cut, align the even horizontal edge of the fabric with the first vertical measurement on the cutting board.

Place the ruler on top so that the measurement you wish to cut is in line with the edge of the fabric; for example, if you wish to cut a 2in (5cm) strip, the 2in (5cm) marking of the ruler will be level with the cut edge of the fabric. Line up the cutter with the ruler and cut away from yourself (3).

It is then easy to cut the strips into shapes for the patchwork pieces.

If you wish to cut squares, place the strip on the cutting board horizontally and then, using the ruler vertically, measure the same width as the strip, keeping a ruler line on the long edge of the strip, ensuring that a right angle is maintained and that you are cross cutting the strip into squares (4). Rectangles can be cut in a similar manner.

To cut right-angled triangles, cut squares as described above, and then cut the squares in half on the diagonal from corner to corner. Make sure that you hold the ruler firmly when cutting on the diagonal as it is easy to wobble and then the triangles will not be consistent in size (5).

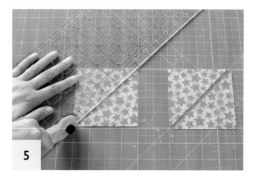

APPLIQUÉ TECHNIQUES

I have used a number of methods for appliqué in these projects. Some methods can be completed on the sewing machine, while others can be sewn by hand. It is up to you which method you prefer to use, or if you are new to appliqué perhaps this is a good opportunity to try out a few before deciding on your favourite. Each technique is described in detail so you simply choose whether you wish to appliqué by machine or hand and then choose the technique to follow from the list.

To machine appliqué using a straight stitch

This is an easy method with fast results. The raw edges of the shapes will fray slightly, creating a soft effect.

Trace the motif onto the paper side of the fusible web. If the motif has several parts, each part must be traced separately **(1)**.

Roughly cut around each traced motif **(2)**.

Place the fusible web motifs onto the reverse of your chosen fabrics so that the paper side is facing you and iron the motif to the fabric **(3)**.

Cut out each motif neatly along the traced lines **(4)**.

Peel the backing paper away from the motif and position it onto your project fabric. Overlap the part motifs where necessary. Iron in place **(5)**.

Using a straight stitch on the sewing machine and a black thread (or a matching thread of your choice), topstitch close to the outer edge of the motifs **(6)**.

For an alternative visual effect, straight stitch around the motifs several times **(7)**.

To machine appliqué using a zigzag stitch

To prepare the motifs, follow the first five stages in the instructions for machine appliqué above, using a straight stitch.

Put the zigzag foot on the sewing machine and change the stitch selector to zigzag. I like to use a more open stitch for the zigzag and match the thread as closely as possible to the fabric to be stitched. This ensures that the stitches sink into the fabric and that the eye is drawn to the motif rather than the stitching **(8)**.

Place the needle of the machine on the fabric, adjacent to the outer edge of the motif, so that the next stitch will go on to the motif. Carefully stitch around the motif, keeping the outer edge of the zigzag stitch adjacent to the very outside edge of the motif at all times **(9)**.

To stitch around a curve, make sure that the needle is down on the outer edge of the motif, raise the foot and slightly turn the fabric, then continue stitching. Do not be tempted to pull the fabric as you stitch as this does not create a smooth curve.

To stitch a corner, stitch to the corner point and ensure that the needle is on the outer point, lift the foot, turn the fabric 90 degrees and continue stitching down the next straight edge. The first few zigzag stitches will overlap the existing stitches **(10)**.

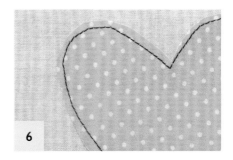

6

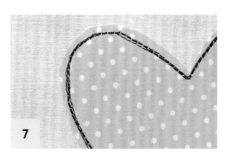

7

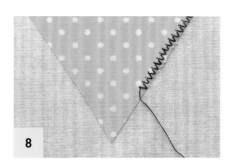

8

9

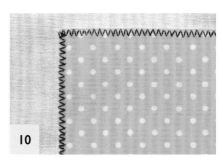

10

To machine appliqué using a blanket stitch

To prepare the motifs, follow the first five stages in the instructions for machine appliqué using a straight stitch.

Put the zigzag foot or open toe foot on the sewing machine and change the stitch selector to blanket stitch. Before starting to blanket stitch around a shape, ensure that the needle of the machine is on the fabric adjacent to the outer edge of the motif so that when you start stitching, the vertical stitch will go into the motif and the following horizontal stitch will sit on the outer edge (11).

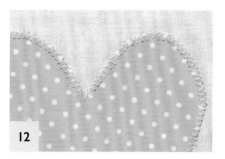

The technique for managing curves and corners is the same as for the zigzag stitch (12).

To hand appliqué using needle turn and freezer paper

Trace the motif on to the matt side of the freezer paper. If the motif has several parts, each must be traced separately. Cut out the freezer paper motif on the drawn lines (13).

Place the motif on the fabric to be appliquéd so the shiny side of the freezer paper is facing the wrong side of the fabric. Iron in place. Cut out the shapes leaving a ¼in (0.65cm) seam allowance of fabric all the way around.

Iron the seam allowance over the outer edge of the freezer paper motif to the reverse of the fabric (14). Carefully remove the freezer paper shapes without disturbing the turned-under outer seam allowances.

Position the motifs on your project fabric and pin in place. Overlap the part motifs where necessary. Using small, neat slip stitches and matching thread, sew the motif to the project fabric along the folded edge (15).

To hand appliqué using a blanket stitch

To prepare the motifs, follow the first five stages in the instructions for machine appliqué using a straight stitch.

Using a matching or contrasting embroidery thread and a blanket stitch, stitch around each motif. To blanket stitch on the raw edge of the fabric, first bring the thread up just below the edge of the fabric and take a diagonal stitch to the right, about ⅛in (0.32cm) in from the fabric edge. Bring the needle out directly below again, just below the edge of the fabric. Loop the thread around the needle where it emerges and pull the thread taut **(16)**.

Continue in this way until the outer edges and any overlapping edges are covered in blanket stitch **(17)**.

16

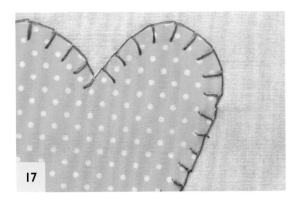

17

PIECING TECHNIQUES

Basic piecing involves stitching two shapes together using a standard straight stitch on the machine. The raw edges of the shapes must be aligned precisely in order for the patchwork to be accurate. A ¼in (0.65cm) seam allowance has been used throughout.

It is important that seams match and points are sharp when piecing. When seams meet at an intersection, make sure that the seam allowances are pressed in opposite directions. The seam allowances should butt together and can be pinned through the stitching lines to hold the pieces in place before stitching.

Pressing

Pressing makes such a difference to the finished product in appliqué and project construction. Good pressing ensures that the shapes lay flat and intersecting seam lines remain smooth.

To steam or not to steam with the iron? Personal preference here, but I always dry iron and never feel the need to use steam.

It is important to iron fabrics before cutting to make sure that all the wrinkles and creases are removed. If you have stubborn creases, such as the line in the centre of fabric where it has been folded around a bolt, spray starch can help eliminate this mark.

All the seams in the project patterns in this book are pressed to one side. The only exception is if there is a very bulky seam, and where this occurs the seams are pressed open. As you complete each stage of the project, it is important to press the seams before moving on to the next step or adding another shape or fabric strip. Each pattern details which direction to press the seams so that in further steps the pieces will butt together. Gently press the seams rather than using a backwards and forwards motion with the iron.

Quilting

Some of the projects in this book have been machine quilted with simple straight or diagonal lines to hold the wadding (batting) to the fabric and/or to add texture. Using a walking foot helps make the quilting easier as the layers are fed through the machine evenly. However, if you do not have a walking foot you can use an ordinary presser foot, but make sure to reduce both the thread tension and foot pressure on the machine to prevent the layers from puckering. It can help to make a sample square of scrap fabric and wadding (batting) to test the settings before starting. I use the same thread in the top and bobbin of my machine, and like to use a 40-weight thread in a colour that complements the fabrics in the quilt. This weight of thread is strong, but fine enough to sink into the quilt layers to create texture.

If you wish to quilt in straight vertical lines, use a fabric marking pencil to draw a line from top to bottom down the centre of the project. Stitch the first line of quilting on this drawn line, then, using the width of the walking foot as a guide, stitch vertical lines moving from the centre out towards the edge.

If you wish to quilt in straight lines on the diagonal, use a fabric marking pencil to draw a line from corner to corner of the project. Stitch on the drawn line, then mark the next diagonal line in parallel to the first and stitch. Repeat across the project.

Binding

When choosing the fabric for the binding you can either use a fabric that is already in the project, which will help to pull the colours together, or a new fabric that complements the project. Some of the projects have been finished with a double fold binding while others have used a bias binding.

To bind the project, trim the excess backing and wadding (batting) level with the edge of the project top. It should be square; if not, use a ruler and rotary cutter to square it up. Stitch the binding strips together to form one continuous strip; this can either be on the straight or at a 45-degree angle. Press seams open to reduce bulk. Fold the strip in half lengthways, wrong sides together, and press. Starting at the top on one side, match the raw edges of the binding to the raw edge of the project and sew in place. Repeat on the other side of the project and then the top and bottom. Finally, fold the binding over to the back of the item and neatly slip stitch in place by hand.

If a project has curved edges it needs to be bound with bias binding, and this will be stated in the pattern instructions. To cut bias strips from fabric, fold the fabric on the diagonal to make a triangle. Cut the strips to the required width across the diagonal, starting at the folded edge. The larger the folded triangle, the longer the bias strips. Strips can be stitched together to get the required length.

FINISHING

Some of the projects require simple hand, machine or a little embroidery stitching to finish. These have been kept to the minimum but do give the project a nice finish.

Topstitching

Many of the projects use topstitching as a decorative feature or to hold fast a finished edge such as the top of a bag or a pocket. Either way, neat and even topstitching helps to improve the appearance of a project and often helps it to lay flat. Each pattern explains what distance the stitched line should be away from the finished edge and usually it is either ⅛in (0.32cm) or ¼in (0.65cm). You can use your standard presser foot on your sewing machine or alternatively a zipper foot or edge stitch foot. The key to neat topstitching is keeping the distance from the finished edge as even as possible.

Slip stitch

A slip stitch is used to secure a finished edge, such as a hand appliquéd shape or binding, invisibly to another fabric. Catch a thread from under the fabric with a needle; at the same time catch a single thread on the fold of the fabric. Repeat, keeping the stitches as even as possible.

Backstitch

This is a strong stitch that can be used either for hand stitching seams or as a decorative stitch to create a solid line. Take a small stitch, bringing the needle point out ⅛in (0.32cm) forward on the line to be stitched. Insert the needle at the end of the last stitch and bring the needle forward again. Stitches are continuous on the right side but overlapped on the wrong side of the fabric.

French knots

These are great little knots that are good for adding features such as eyes or dots to projects. To stitch a French knot, pass your threaded needle through the fabric from back to front. A standard French knot generally has the thread wrapped around the needle twice. Start with your needle closest to you and the thread behind it. Wrap the thread around the needle towards yourself twice, keeping the thread tight as you do so. Pass your needle back through your fabric from front to back. While holding the thread tightly, turn your needle downward and pick a point as close to your original starting point as possible, **without using the same hole**. Pull the needle all the way back through your fabric, and slowly pull through the remaining thread.

Example shows French knot and backstitch technique

NEEDLE CASE

Store your needles and pins in style in this compact needle case, decorated with a cute sewing machine motif. With its felt insert, it is particularly useful when taking sewing projects out and about. Team it up with the pincushion (see page 24) and button bag (see page 28) to make the perfect gift for a sewing friend.

SKILL LEVEL: EASY

YOU'LL NEED

FABRIC

Requirements based on fabrics with a useable width of 42in (107cm):

- 5in (12.7cm) beige for the outer needle case

- 5in (12.7cm) pink print for the inner needle case

- Small fabric scraps in pink, beige and red for the appliqué

WADDING (BATTING)

- 9½ x 5in (24 x 12.7cm) fusible wadding (batting)

HABERDASHERY

- Neutral thread for piecing

- 12in (30.5cm) length of pink ribbon, ⅛in (0.32cm) wide

- 8 x 3½in (20.3 x 8.9cm) pink felt for the inside

- One small pink button

Tips

When you get to Step 4, tuck the ribbon in towards the middle of the case so it does not get caught in the seam.

If you wish to add a further page to your needle case, sew in a second piece of felt when you get to Step 7.

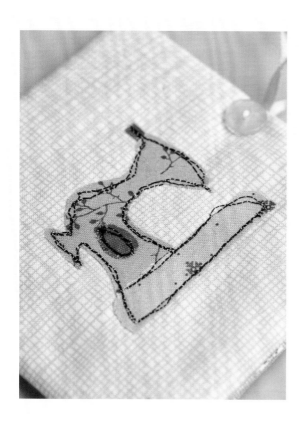

NEEDLE CASE

Size: 4½ × 9in (11.5 × 23cm)

PREPARATION

The outer needle case is constructed with an appliquéd sewing machine on the front and a plain back, while the inside contains a felt insert for storing needles and pins. It is finished with a ribbon and button tie.

CUTTING

All cutting instructions include a ¼in (0.65cm) seam allowance.

Beige fabric
• One 9½ × 5in (24 × 12.7cm) rectangle

Pink print fabric
• One 9½ × 5in (24 × 12.7cm) rectangle

Fabric scraps
• One sewing machine motif (see page 138)

Fusible wadding (batting)
• One 9½ × 5in (24 × 12.7cm) rectangle

Pink felt
• One 8 × 3½in (20.3 × 8.9cm) rectangle

METHOD

To stitch the appliqué:

1 Fold the beige rectangle in half to determine the centre of the front square for the motif. Appliqué the sewing machine to the beige rectangle, positioning the bottom of the machine 1¼in (3.1cm) up from the bottom of the fabric. This project has been appliquéd using straight stitch machine appliqué (see page 13). Press well.

To stitch the needle case together:

2 Iron the fusible wadding (batting) to the wrong side of the beige appliquéd fabric completed in Step 1.

3 Place it on a surface with the right side facing up, then fold the ribbon in half and pin the folded end in the middle of the side at the opposite end to the appliqué. Stitch the ribbon in place ⅛in (0.32cm) from the edge.

4 With right sides together, pin the outer unit on top of the 9½ x 5in (24 x 12.7cm) pink print rectangle and stitch around each side, leaving a 2in (5cm) gap in the stitching in the middle of one of the long sides.

To finish the needle case:

5 Trim the corners and turn the needle case through the gap so it is right side out. Push out the corners and give it a press. Close the opening with small, neat slip stitches.

6 Lay the 8 x 3½in (20.3 x 8.9cm) felt rectangle on the inside of the needle case and pin it in the centre. Sew a single line of stitching down through the centre. This should line up with the seam in the centre front. Stitch the button to the front of the case, aligning it with the ribbon. To close, bring the ribbon around the front and tie in a bow.

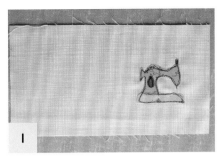

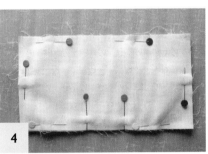

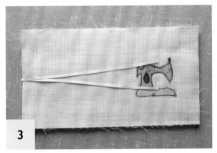

PINCUSHION

An essential piece of equipment for anyone who sews, this pincushion is large enough to store all your pins. With its super-stylish cotton reel motifs, it's also one you will be pleased to leave out on display. Make it with the needle case (see page 20) and button bag (see page 28) for the perfect sewing-themed trio.

SKILL LEVEL: EASY

YOU'LL NEED

FABRIC

Requirements based on fabrics with a useable width of 42in (107cm):

- 4in (10cm) beige for the top of the pincushion

- 4in (10cm) pink spot for the back of the pincushion

- Small fabric scraps in brown and pink stripes for the appliqué

HABERDASHERY

- Neutral thread for piecing

- Polyester toy filling

Tip

I have stuffed my pincushion with polyester toy filling, but if you prefer you can buy a special heavier stuffing for pincushions, which helps to keep the pins sharp.

PINCUSHION

Size: 3½ × 6½in (8.9 × 16.5cm)

PREPARATION

The pincushion has three appliquéd cotton reels on the front and a spotty fabric back.

CUTTING

All cutting instructions include a ¼in (0.65cm) seam allowance.

Beige fabric
• One 7 × 4in (17.8 × 10cm) rectangle

Pink spot fabric
• One 7 × 4in (17.8 × 10cm) rectangle

Fabric scraps
• Three cotton reel motifs (see page 138)

METHOD

. . . .

To stitch the appliqué:

1 Appliqué the cotton reels to the beige rectangle, positioning them so they are ½in (1.3cm) from the outer edge of the fabric. This project has been appliquéd using straight stitch machine appliqué (see page 13).

To stitch the pincushion together:

2 With right sides together, pin the 7 × 4in (17.8 × 10cm) pink spot rectangle on top of the unit completed in Step 1.

3 Stitch around each side, leaving a 2in (5cm) gap in the stitching in the middle of one of the long sides.

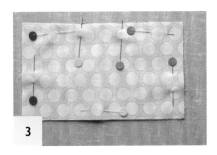

To finish the pincushion:

4 Trim the corners and turn the pincushion through the gap so that it is right side out. Stuff with the polyester toy filling, pushing it in firmly.

5 Close the opening with small, neat slip stitches.

Tip

You could reduce the number of cotton reels on the top to two, to allow for more of the background fabric to be seen.

BUTTON BAG

Store your button collection in this pretty but practical bag, suitably decorated with real and appliquéd buttons! This dainty bag is portable, so is great for finding your favourite button when stitching on the go. It goes perfectly with the needle case (see page 20) and pincushion (see page 24) to make a lovely sewing-themed set.

SKILL LEVEL: EASY

YOU'LL NEED

FABRIC

Requirements based on fabrics with a useable width of 42in (107cm):

- 6in (15.2cm) beige for the outer bag

- 3½in (8.9cm) pink floral for the top of the outer bag

- 8½in (21.6cm) pink print for the lining

- Small fabric scraps in light and dark pink for the appliqué

HABERDASHERY

- Neutral thread for piecing

- Black embroidery thread

- Seven assorted pink buttons

- 24in (61cm) cream ribbon, ½in (1.3cm) wide

Tips

After sewing the ribbon to the outer section, fold it up and pin it to the fabric before stitching the outer units together. This will ensure that the ribbon does not get caught in the stitching.

Don't choose a heavily patterned lining fabric – it will make it more difficult to find the button you want in the bag.

BUTTON BAG

Size: 8 × 8¼in (20.3 × 21cm)

PREPARATION:

The outer button bag has appliquéd and real buttons on its front with a contrast fabric top. The bag is fully lined with a ribbon trim for gathering the top.

CUTTING

All cutting instructions include a ¼in (0.65cm) seam allowance.

Beige fabric
• Two 8½ × 6in (21.6 × 15.2cm) rectangles

Pink floral fabric
• Two 8½ × 3¼in (21.6 × 8.2cm) rectangles

Pink print fabric
• Two 8½ × 8½in (21.6 × 21.6cm) squares

Fabric scraps
• Five button motifs (see page 138)

METHOD

To assemble the button bag:

1 Stitch an 8½ x 3¼in (21.6 x 8.2cm) pink floral rectangle to the top of each 8½ x 6in (21.6 x 15.2cm) beige rectangle. Press the seam towards the beige fabric.

To stitch the appliqué:

2 Take one of the units completed in Step 1 and appliqué the button motifs to the beige fabric, positioning the buttons 1in (2.5cm) up from the bottom and 2in (5cm) in from each side of the fabric. This project has been appliquéd using needle turn hand appliqué (see page 15). Using the black embroidery thread, stitch some French knots and little crosses to the centre of each motif.

3 Stitch the seven buttons randomly around the appliquéd button motifs.

To stitch the button bag together:

4 Fold the ribbon in half and place it on the right side of the second unit completed in Step 1, positioning the centre of the ribbon on the centre of the seam line between the pink floral and beige fabric. Stitch across the width of the ribbon at this centre point.

5 Pin the two outer units right side together and stitch up each side and across the bottom. Trim corners. Repeat with the two 8½ x 8½in (21.6 x 21.6cm) pink print squares to make the lining, but leave a 2½in (6.3cm) opening in the middle of one side.

To finish the button bag:

6 Turn through the outer button bag so that the right side is facing out. Place it inside the lining, right sides together, and pin all the way around the top edge. Sew around this edge, matching the side seams.

7 Turn the bag right side out through the opening in the lining. Stitch the opening closed and press well. Topstitch ⅛in (0.32cm) around the top of the bag. Place your buttons in the bag and tie the ribbon with a neat bow.

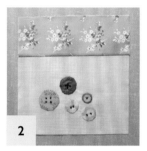

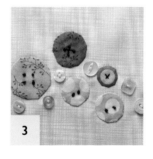
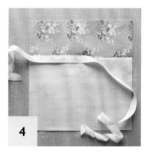

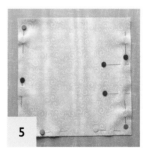
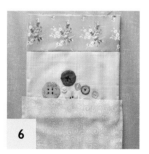

NOTEBOOK COVER

Turn an ordinary notebook into a treasured possession with this fun pencil-themed cover. The beauty of making your own cover is that once your notebook is full of lists, recipes or notes, you can simply take it off and reuse it on your next one. Team it with the pencil case (see page 36) for a smart matching set.

SKILL LEVEL: EASY

YOU'LL NEED

FABRIC

Requirements based on fabrics with a useable width of 42in (107cm):

- 10in (25cm) cream print for the notebook outer

- 10in (25cm) patterned print for the lining and inner flaps

- Fabric scraps in red, blue, yellow, pink, turquoise and peach for the appliqué

HABERDASHERY

- Neutral thread for piecing

- 10in (25cm) fusible interfacing

- 6 x 8½in (15.2 x 21.6cm) notebook

Tip

The instructions can be adjusted to make a cover to fit a different sized notebook. To do this, measure the width of the notebook including the front, moving around the spine and then to the back. Add 1in (2.5cm) to this measurement. Measure the height of the notebook and add 1in (2.5cm) to this measurement. This gives you the cutting measurements for the front cover, lining and interfacing. To calculate the flaps, use the same height measurement as the front cover and keep the width the same as the pattern.

NOTEBOOK COVER

Size: 6¼ × 8¾in (15.8 × 22.2cm)

PREPARATION

The notebook cover has five appliquéd pencils on the front cover and a contrast lining with a flap each side to tuck around the notebook.

CUTTING

All cutting instructions include a ¼in (0.65cm) seam allowance.

Cream fabric
• One 13½ × 9½in (34.3 × 24cm) rectangle

Patterned print
• One 13½ × 9½in (34.3 × 24cm) rectangle

• Two 7½ × 9½in (19 × 24cm) rectangles

Fabric scraps
• Five pencil motifs (see page 138)

Fusible interfacing
• One 13½ × 9½in (34.3 × 24cm) rectangle

METHOD

To stitch the appliqué:

1 Fold the cream rectangle in half to determine the centre front for the motifs. Appliqué the pencils to the cream rectangle, positioning them in a random arrangement across half of the rectangle. Ensure that the pencils are positioned at least ¾in (1.9cm) in from any outer edge. This project has been appliquéd using straight stitch machine appliqué (see page 13).

To stitch the notebook cover together:

2 Iron the fusible interfacing to the reverse of the unit completed in Step 1.

3 To make the inner flaps, fold each of the 7½ × 9½in (19 × 24cm) patterned rectangles in half vertically, wrong sides together, and press. Place an inner flap on each end of the right side of the notebook cover, so that the raw edges line up and the folded edge faces the centre, and pin around the outer edges.

4 Lay the 13½ × 9½in (34.3 × 24cm) patterned rectangle on top of the cover, right sides together. Pin around the outer edge, then stitch around all four sides, leaving a 3in (7.5cm) opening in the stitching on one long side. Trim corners.

To finish the notebook cover:

5 Turn the cover through the gap so that it is right side out. Push out the corners and give it a press. Close the opening with small, neat slip stitches and place on your notebook.

PENCIL CASE

Store and protect your stationery with this stylish pencil case, decorated with eye-catching appliquéd pencils. The zipped top gives the case a practical finish, ensuring that all your pens and pencils stay in one place. Coupled with the matching notebook cover (see page 32), this would make a great gift for a student.

SKILL LEVEL: REQUIRES EXPERIENCE

YOU'LL NEED

FABRIC
Requirements based on fabrics with a useable width of 42in (107cm):

* 10in (25cm) cream print for the outer case

* 10in (25cm) navy for the inner case

* Fabric scraps in red, blue, yellow, pink, turquoise and peach for the appliqué

HABERDASHERY

* Neutral thread for piecing

* 10in (25cm) fusible interfacing

* 9in (22.9cm) beige metal zip

Tips

It is really important to open the zip halfway in Step 5. If you forget, you will be unable to turn the pencil case out to the right side.

It is a good idea to use a dark fabric for the lining, as this will help to hide any marks that pencils may make to the inside of the pencil case.

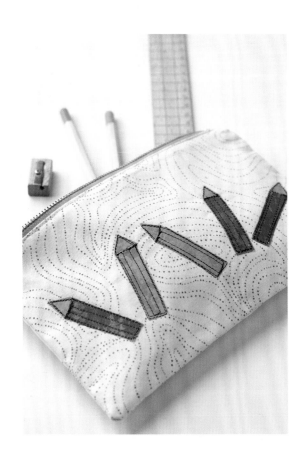

PENCIL CASE

Size: 5½ × 9in (14 × 22.9cm)

PREPARATION

The pencil case has appliquéd pencils on the outside with a plain dark lining. The use of the metal zip and interfacing ensures that the pencil case is robust.

CUTTING

All cutting instructions include a ¼in (0.65cm) seam allowance.

Cream fabric
- Two 9½ × 6in (24 × 15.2cm) rectangles

Navy fabric
- Two 9½ × 5¾in (24 × 14.6cm) rectangles

Fabric scraps
- Five pencil motifs (see page 138)

Fusible interfacing
- Two 9½ × 6in (24 × 15.2cm) rectangles

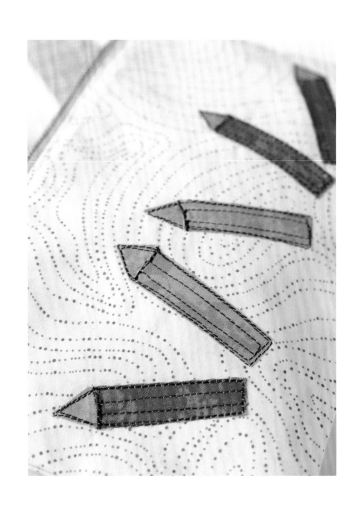

METHOD

To stitch the appliqué:

1 Appliqué the pencil motifs to one of the 9½ × 6in (24 × 15.2cm) cream rectangles, positioning them in a random arrangement across the rectangle. This project has been appliquéd using straight stitch machine appliqué (see page 13). Iron the fusible interfacing to the reverse of this unit.

To attach the zip:

2 Place the first outer case section right side up and place the zip face down on front of it, matching the top edge. Pin along the top of the zip. Place a 9½ × 5¾in (24 × 14.6cm) navy rectangle on top, right side down, and stitch along the top edge to secure the lining, zip and outer case.

3 Repeat Step 2 to attach the zip to the second case section, then open out each panel and press.

4 Topstitch ⅛in (0.32cm) each side of the zip.

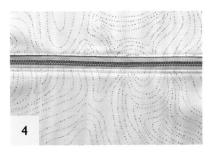

To stitch the pencil case together:

5 Open the zip halfway. Place the two outer case sections right side together, and the lining panels right sides together. Pin and stitch all the way around the edge, leaving a 2in (5cm) gap in the stitching at the bottom of the lining.

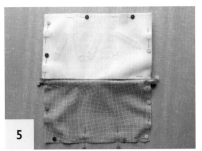

To finish the pencil case:

6 Turn the case through the opening in the lining so it is right side out. Push out the corners and give it a press. Stitch the opening closed with small, neat slip stitches.

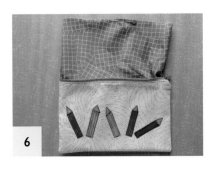

TABLET CASE

Keep your tablet or mini laptop safe when out and about with this softly padded case. The stylish appliquéd circles and boldly coloured fabrics will ensure you stand out from the crowd! The case is quilted, which not only gives it texture but helps increase its padding, making sure your device is protected.

SKILL LEVEL: REQUIRES EXPERIENCE

YOU'LL NEED

FABRIC

Requirements based on fabrics with a useable width of 42in (107cm):

- 12in (30.5cm) pink print for the outer case and flap

- 12in (30.5cm) patterned print for the inner case and circle motifs

WADDING (BATTING)

- 12in (30.5cm) fusible wadding (batting)

HABERDASHERY

- Neutral thread for piecing

- Pink thread for quilting

- 2in (5cm) strip of hook and loop sew-on tape, 1in (2.5cm) wide

Tips

The size of the tablet case can be adjusted to fit a device of any size. Simply measure the width and length of your tablet and add 2in (5cm) to these measurements. Keep the flap measurement the same.

You could make the tablet case in a fabric that coordinates with the pencil case and notebook to create a matching set.

TABLET CASE

Size: 9½ × 11½in (24 × 29cm)

PREPARATION

The tablet case has appliquéd circles on the front, a contrast lining, which creates a border around the opening, and a fold-over flap. It is padded with wadding (batting).

CUTTING

All cutting instructions include a ¼in (0.65cm) seam allowance.

Pink fabric
- Two 12 × 10in (30.5 × 25cm) rectangles
- Two 5in (12.7cm) squares

Patterned print
- Two 12 × 10in (30.5 × 25cm) rectangles
- Five circle motifs in various sizes (see page 138)

Fusible wadding (batting)
- Two 12 × 10in (30.5 × 25cm) rectangles
- One 5in (12.7cm) square

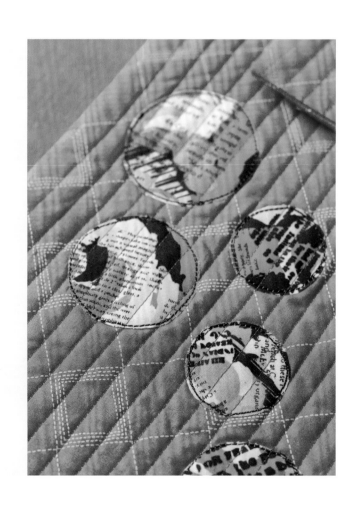

METHOD

To stitch the appliqué:

1 Take one of the 12 × 10in (30.5 × 25cm) pink rectangles and appliqué five circle motifs to the fabric, positioning them randomly and ensuring that they are not placed in the top 4in (10cm) section of the fabric. The 10in (25cm) side is at the top. This project has been appliquéd using straight stitch machine appliqué (see page 13).

To stitch the tablet case together:

2 Iron the fusible wadding (batting) to the wrong side of the unit completed in Step 1, the remaining 12 × 10in (30.5 × 25cm) pink rectangle and to one of the 5in (12.7cm) pink squares.

3 Quilt vertical lines from top to bottom through both the fabric and wadding (batting), ½in (1.3cm) apart across all units.

4 Pull the hook and loop tape apart and stitch one side of the tape to the pink appliquéd rectangle, positioning the tape 1¾in (4.4cm) from the top of the unit in the centre. Stitch around all four sides to secure.

5 Place the two quilted 12 × 10in (30.5 × 25cm) pink rectangles right sides together, pin and stitch up each long side and across one short side. Trim corners and turn through.

6 To make the flap, stitch the second piece of hook and loop tape to the right side of the remaining 5in (12.7cm) pink square, positioning the tape ½in (1.3cm) up from the outer edge in the centre of one side.

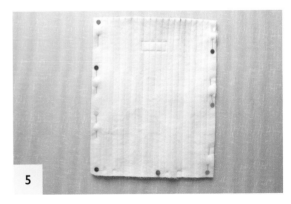

7 Place the two flap units right sides together and stitch around three sides. The side with the hook and loop tape should be at the bottom. Trim corners, turn through and press.

8 With quilted sides facing, pin and stitch the flap unit completed in Step 7 to the centre of the top edge of the back of the outer case completed in Step 5.

9 To make the inner case, place the two 12 × 10in (30.5 × 25cm) patterned rectangles right sides together and stitch up each long side and across one short side, leaving a 3in (7.5cm) gap in the stitching in the middle of one side.

To finish the tablet case:

10 Place the outer tablet case, right side facing out, inside the lining, right sides together. Pin all the way around the top edge, matching the side seams. Turn the case right side out through the opening in the lining. Stitch the opening closed with small, neat slip stitches.

11 Carefully press the top of the tablet case so that ¼in (0.65cm) of the lining is showing on the outside and pin in place. Stitch through all layers in the seam line around the top.

7

8

9

10

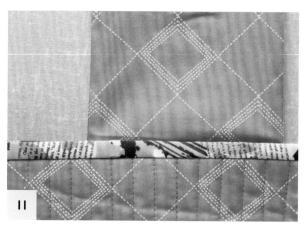

11

COFFEE COSY

Who doesn't love a cup of coffee to start the day? This cheerful cosy wraps around the cafetière to keep your coffee piping hot, giving you plenty of opportunity for that second or third cup! Decorated with cute coffee cups against a bright yellow background, it is sure to brighten up your breakfast table.

SKILL LEVEL: EASY

YOU'LL NEED

FABRIC
Requirements based on fabrics with a useable width of 42in (107cm):

- 5in (12.7cm) yellow spot for the outer cosy

- 5in (12.7cm) green check for the lining

- Fabric scraps in red and brown for the appliqué

WADDING (BATTING)

- 5in (12.7cm) fusible wadding (batting)

HABERDASHERY

- Neutral thread for piecing

- 3½in (8.9cm) strip sew-on hook and loop tape, 1in (2.5cm) wide

Tips

I have used fusible wadding (batting) for my cosy, but for additional warmth you could use an insulated version instead.

The measurements for this coffee cosy fit a six-cup cafetière with the edges overlapping by 1½in (4cm), which gives the cover a snug fit. Before starting the project, measure your cafetière to ensure that the cover will fit. If it doesn't, adjust the measurements accordingly.

COFFEE COSY

Size: 13½ × 4¼in (34.3 × 10.8cm)

PREPARATION

The coffee cosy has three appliquéd coffee cups on the outer and is lined with wadding (batting) and a backing fabric. The cosy is fixed around the cafetière with a hook and loop fixing.

CUTTING

All cutting instructions include a ¼in (0.65cm) seam allowance.

Yellow fabric
• One 14 × 4¾in (35.8 × 12cm) rectangle

Green fabric
• One 14 × 4¾in (35.8 × 12cm) rectangle

Fabric scraps
• Three coffee cup motifs (see page 139)

Fusible wadding (batting)
• One 14 × 4¾in (35.8 × 12cm) rectangle

METHOD

. . . .

To stitch the appliqué:

1 Appliqué the coffee cups to the 14 x 4¾in (35.8 x 12cm) yellow rectangle, positioning the cups in a random arrangement across the rectangle. Ensure that the cups are 1in (2.5cm) away from the outer long edges and 2½in (6.3cm) away from the short edges. This project has been appliquéd using blanket stitch machine appliqué (see page 15).

To stitch the coffee cosy together:

2 Take half of the hook and loop tape and stitch it to the left side of the 14 x 4¾in (35.8 x 12cm) green rectangle, ½in (1.3cm) in from the edge of one short end.

3 Iron the fusible wadding (batting) to the wrong side of the green rectangle.

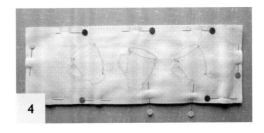

4 With right sides together, place the unit completed in Step 1 on top of the unit completed in Step 3, pin and stitch around each side, leaving a 2in (5cm) gap in the stitching on one long edge. Trim corners.

5 Turn the cosy through the gap so it is right side out. Press carefully and topstitch around each side, ¼in (0.65cm) in from the edge, closing the opening as you go.

To finish the coffee cosy:

6 Stitch the second half of the hook and loop tape to the short edge of the outer cosy, on the opposite end to the other strip of tape.

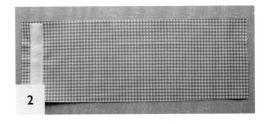

EGG COSIES

What came first, the chicken or the egg? Keep your boiled eggs warm and toasty under these adorable little egg cosies in springtime colours, decorated with cute appliqué chickens. Children will love them and they are guaranteed to bring a smile to your face at mealtimes.

SKILL LEVEL: EASY

YOU'LL NEED

FABRIC

The fabric requirements allow for two cosies.

Requirements based on fabrics with a useable width of 42in (107cm):

- 4in (10cm) green check for the outer cosies
- 4in (10cm) yellow spot for the lining
- Fabric scraps in yellow and orange for the motifs

WADDING (BATTING)

- 4in (10cm) fusible wadding (batting)

HABERDASHERY

- Neutral thread for piecing
- Black embroidery thread
- 6in (15.2cm) yellow ribbon, ½in (1.3cm) wide

Tip

This is a great little scrap-busting project – each cosy could be stitched in different scraps of fabric.

These could be stitched at Easter time and given as gifts over small chocolate eggs.

EGG COSIES

Size: 3 × 3in (7.5 × 7.5cm)

PREPARATION

Each egg cosy features an appliquéd chicken, is fully lined, has wadding (batting) inside on the front and is finished with a ribbon pull on the top.

CUTTING

All cutting instructions include a ¼in (0.65cm) seam allowance.

Green fabric
- Using the cosy template (see page 139), cut four shapes

Yellow fabric
- Using the cosy template (see page 139), cut four shapes

Fabric scraps
- Two chicken motifs (see page 139)

Fusible wadding (batting)
- Using the cosy template, cut two shapes

METHOD

To stitch the appliqué:

1 Appliqué a chicken motif on two of the green cosy shapes, ensuring that each one is placed in the centre. Embroider an eye with a French knot and add legs using backstitch. This project has been appliquéd using blanket stitch machine appliqué (see page 15).

To stitch the egg cosies together:

2 Iron the fusible wadding (batting) to the wrong side of both the units completed in Step 1.

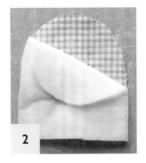

3 Cut the ribbon into two 3in (7.5cm) strips and fold each strip in half. Placing the raw edges together, stitch the ends of the ribbon to the centre top of each of the units completed in Step 2. Stitch with a ⅛in (0.32cm) seam.

4 Place the two outer egg cosy sections right sides together. Pin and stitch around the curved edge, leaving the straight side open. Clip curves. Turn right side out and press.

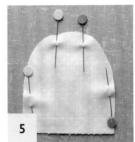

5 To stitch the lining, pin the two yellow lining sections right sides together and stitch around the curved edge, leaving a 1in (2.5cm) gap in the stitching in the centre top. Clip curves.

To finish the egg cosies:

6 Place the outer cosy inside the lining, right sides together, and pin around the edge. Stitch together, matching the side seams. Turn the egg cosy right side out through the gap and stitch the opening closed. Press.

BREAD BASKET

Nothing beats the smell of fresh bread in the kitchen! This colourful bread basket will brighten up any table setting and is roomy enough to be filled with several warm bread rolls. I have made mine to match the egg cosies (see page 50) and coffee cosy (see page 46) to give a coordinated feel to my home.

SKILL LEVEL: REQUIRES EXPERIENCE

YOU'LL NEED

FABRIC

Requirements based on fabrics with a useable width of 42in (107cm):

Please note that this project is not suitable for fabrics with directional prints

- 20in (50.8cm) yellow spot for the outer basket

- 20in (50.8cm) green check for the inner basket and appliqué motif

- Fabric scrap in red print for the appliqué motif

WADDING (BATTING)

- 20in (50.8cm) fusible wadding (batting)

HABERDASHERY

- Neutral thread for piecing

> **Tips**
>
> I have made my basket using fusible wadding (batting) but to keep your bread warm you could use an insulated version instead.
>
> The appliquéd motif could be added to the back of the basket as well, if desired.

BREAD BASKET

Size: 7½ × 6½in (19 × 16.5cm)

PREPARATION

The bread basket is made from two pieces of contrasting fabric with an appliquéd jar of jam on the front of the basket. It is lined with fusible wadding for stability.

CUTTING

All cutting instructions include a ¼in (0.65cm) seam allowance.

Yellow fabric
- One 20 × 14½in (50.8 × 37cm) rectangle

Green fabric
- One 19 × 14½in (48.3 × 37cm) rectangle
- One jar lid motif (see page 139)

Fabric scrap
- One jar motif (see page 139)

Fusible wadding (batting)
- One 20 × 14½in (50.8 × 37cm) rectangle

METHOD

To stitch the appliqué:

1 Position the bottom of the appliqué jam jar in the centre of the yellow rectangle, 5in (12.7cm) from the 14½in (37cm) edge. The top of the jar should be closest to the raw edge of the fabric. This project has been appliquéd using blanket stitch hand appliqué (see page 16).

To stitch the bread basket together:

2 Iron the fusible wadding (batting) to the wrong side of the unit completed in Step 1.

3 Fold the basket in half with right sides together, with the 14½in (37cm) opening at the top, pin and stitch down each side.

4 To shape the base, match the centre base line with the side seam. Measure in 3½in (8.9cm) along the seam line and stitch across. Cut off the excess fabric. Repeat on the opposite corner.

5 To stitch the inner basket, take the 19 × 14½in (48.3 × 37cm) green rectangle and fold in half, right sides facing, with the 14½in (37cm) opening at the top. Pin and stitch down each side, leaving a 2½in (6.3cm) gap in the stitching on one side.

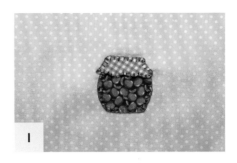

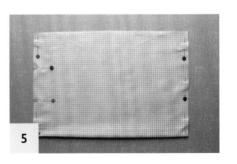

6 To shape the inner base, repeat the instructions in Step 4 with the unit completed in Step 5.

To finish the bread basket:

7 Turn the outer basket through and place inside the inner basket so that right sides are facing. Pin around the top, matching the side seams, and then stitch all the way round.

8 Turn the basket through the gap in the stitching. Push out the corners and stitch the gap closed using small, neat slip stitches. Press and topstitch around the edge ⅛in (0.32cm) in from the top. Fold the inner basket 1in (2.5cm) over the top of the outer basket.

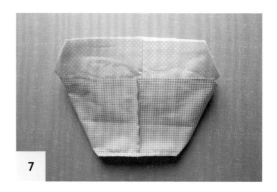

PLACEMATS

These fresh and funky apple-themed placemats are super practical. Suitable for both indoor or outdoor entertaining, they will brighten up every table setting and are washable, so you don't have to worry about those crumbs and spills! I have sewn them as a set of two, but more could be made for extra guests.

SKILL LEVEL: EASY

YOU'LL NEED

FABRIC
Requirements based on fabrics with a useable width of 42in (107cm):

- 20in (50.8cm) green spot for the top of the placemats and binding

- 20in (50.8cm) red check for the contrast panel and backing

- Fabric scraps in brown, green and green print for the appliqué

WADDING (BATTING)
- 20in (50.8cm) fusible wadding (batting)

HABERDASHERY
- Neutral thread for piecing

- Green thread for quilting

Tips

The number of appliquéd apples could be reduced on each placemat to create more negative space, if desired.

Insulated heat-resistant wadding (batting) could be substituted if the mats were to be used for oven-to-table dishes.

PLACEMATS

Size: 15½ × 12½in (39.4 × 31.7cm)

PREPARATION

The fabric requirements allow for two placemats. Each placemat has a contrast panel featuring four appliquéd apples. The mats are padded with wadding (batting) and finished with bound edges.

CUTTING

All cutting instructions include a ¼in (0.65cm) seam allowance.

Green spot fabric

- Two 12½in (31.7cm) squares

- Three 2in (5cm) widths of fabric strips

Red check fabric

- Two 15½in × 12½in (39.4 × 31.7cm) rectangles

- Two 12½ × 3½in (31.7 × 8.9cm) rectangles

Fabric scraps

- Eight apple, leaf and stalk motifs (see page 139)

Fusible wadding (batting):

- Two 15½in × 12½in (39.4 × 31.7cm) rectangles

METHOD
(TO MAKE ONE PLACEMAT)

To stitch the appliqué:

1 Take a 12½ x 3½in (31.7 x 8.9cm) red rectangle and appliqué four apple motifs to the fabric, positioning them in a vertical line and ensuring that they are placed ½in (1.3cm) in from the outer raw edges. This project has been appliquéd using zigzag stitch machine appliqué (see page 14).

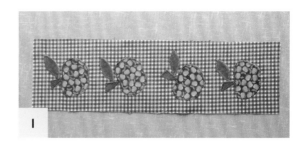

To stitch the placemat together:

2 Stitch the appliquéd red rectangle to the 12½in (31.7cm) green square. Press the seam towards the green square.

3 Iron the fusible wadding (batting) to the wrong side of the unit completed in Step 2. Place this on top of the wrong side of the 15½ x 12½in (39.4 x 31.7cm) red rectangle. Secure the placemat sandwich with tacking (basting) stitches or pin at regular intervals.

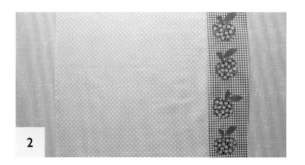

4 Using the green thread, machine quilt diagonal lines 3in (7.5cm) apart across the placemat in both directions.

To finish the placemat:

5 Stitch the three green 2in (5cm) width of fabric strips together to form one continuous strip. Press seams open to reduce bulk. Fold the strip in half lengthwise, wrong sides together, and press. Only half of this strip will be needed for the placement; the remainder is to be saved for the second mat. Match the raw edges of the binding to the raw edges of the placemat and sew in place.

6 Fold the binding over to the back of the placemat, pin in place and neatly slip stitch in place by hand. Give the placemat a final press.

TEA COSY

Keep your teapot nice and toasty with this delightful tea cosy. Not only will it keep your tea piping hot, but it will add a touch of glamour to your kitchen at the same time. I have made my tea cosy to match the coasters (see page 70) to bring a bright and colourful coordinated look to any tea party!

SKILL LEVEL: EASY

YOU'LL NEED

FABRIC
Requirements based on fabrics with a useable width of 42in (107cm):

- 15in (38cm) floral for the outer tea cosy
- 15in (38cm) turquoise for the lining
- Fabric scraps in pink and yellow for the motifs

WADDING (BATTING)
- 15in (38cm) fusible wadding (batting)

HABERDASHERY
- Neutral thread for piecing
- Turquoise thread for quilting

Tips

An extra appliquéd teapot motif could be stitched to the second outer side so that the tea cosy is the same on both sides.

The tea cosy is reversible, so could be used inside out, if required.

TEA COSY

Size: 16 × 11½in (40.6 × 29cm)

PREPARATION

The tea cosy has an appliquéd teapot on one side, is quilted with vertical stitching and is fully lined with a shaped top.

CUTTING

All cutting instructions include a ¼in (0.65cm) seam allowance.

Floral fabric

- Two 16½ × 12in (42 × 30cm) rectangles

Turquoise fabric

- Two 16½ × 12in (42 × 30cm) rectangles

Fabric scraps

- One teapot motif (see page 140)

Fusible wadding (batting)

- Two 16½ × 12in (42 × 30cm) rectangles

METHOD

To shape the top of the tea cosy:

1 Take one 16½ × 12in (42 × 30cm) floral rectangle. Measure 5in (12.7cm) down from the corner on one side and mark the point. Then measure 5in (12.7cm) along the top from the same corner and mark this point. Using a plate or circle template, draw a curve from point to point. Use scissors to cut along the curve. Repeat on the opposite corner. Repeat on the second outer rectangle, both turquoise lining rectangles and both pieces of wadding (batting).

To stitch the appliqué:

2 Appliqué the teapot motif to the centre of one of the outer tea cosy units. This project has been stitched using zigzag stitch machine appliqué (see page 14).

To stitch the tea cosy together:

3 Iron the fusible wadding (batting) to the wrong side of both outer units.

4 Quilt vertical lines from top to bottom at 2in (5cm) intervals using the turquoise thread.

5 Place the two outer tea cosy units together. Pin and stitch up each short side and along the curved top. Clip curves. Turn right side out and press.

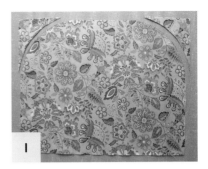

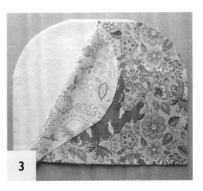

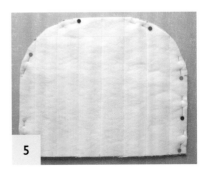

6 To stitch the inner lining units together, place the two 16½ × 12in (42 × 30cm) turquoise curved top rectangles right sides together. Pin and stitch up each short side and along the curved top. Leave a 4in (10.2cm) gap in the stitching in the centre top. Clip curves.

To finish the tea cosy:

7 Place the outer cosy inside the lining, right sides together, and pin all the way around the edge. Stitch together, matching the side seams.

8 Turn the cosy right side out through the gap and stitch the opening closed using small, neat slip stitches. Carefully press the cosy and then topstitch ¼in (0.65cm) away from the bottom outer edge.

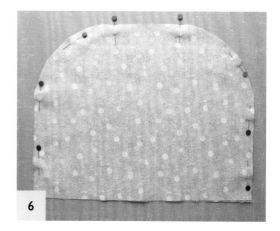

COASTERS

These bright and bold coasters are ever so practical as they are washable and handy for protecting the table from coffee rings. I have made a set of two to match the tea cosy (see page 64), but it is easy to make more if you are entertaining a crowd.

SKILL LEVEL: EASY

YOU'LL NEED

FABRIC

Requirements based on fabrics with a useable width of 42in (107cm):

- 5in (12.7cm) floral for the top and backing

- Fabric scraps in pink and yellow for the appliqué

HABERDASHERY

- 5in (12.7cm) medium-weight fusible interfacing

- Neutral thread for piecing

- Grey thread for topstitching

Tips

If you require the coaster inner to be more substantial you could choose to use a thicker interfacing.

Extra coasters could be stitched and personalized with alternative cup or mug designs to create a designer set.

COASTERS

Size: 4in (10cm) square

PREPARATION

The fabric requirements allow for two coasters. Each coaster has an appliquéd cup on one side and is lined with interfacing.

CUTTING

All cutting instructions include a ¼in (0.65cm) seam allowance.

Floral fabric
- Four 4½in (11.5cm) squares

Fabric scraps
- Two cup motifs (see page 139)

Fusible interfacing
- Two 4½in (11.5cm) squares

METHOD
(TO MAKE ONE COASTER)

To stitch the appliqué:

1 Appliqué the cup to the centre of one 4½in (11.5cm) floral square. This project has been appliquéd using zigzag stitch machine appliqué (see page 14).

To stitch the coaster together:

2 Iron a 4½in (11.5cm) square of interfacing to the wrong side of the unit completed in Step 1.

3 Place the unit completed in Step 2 on top of a 4½in (11.5cm) floral square, right sides together. Pin and stitch around each side, leaving a 1½in (3.8cm) gap in the stitching on one side.

4 Trim corners and turn through. Press carefully.

To finish the coaster:

5 Using the grey thread, topstitch around the outer edge, ⅛in (0.32cm) away from the edge, closing the side opening as you go.

SCENTED SLEEP PILLOW

Put this little lavender-filled pillow on your bed at night and its soothing scent will help you get a good night's sleep. Not only does this pillow smell wonderful, it is quick to make and looks really stylish with its appliquéd hearts and gentle patchwork.

SKILL LEVEL: EASY

YOU'LL NEED

FABRIC
Requirements based on fabrics with a useable width of 42in (107cm):

- 9in (23cm) peach for the patchwork and pillow back

- 4in (10cm) pink for the patchwork and appliqué motifs

HABERDASHERY
- Neutral thread for piecing

- Polyester toy filling

- 1oz (25g) dried lavender or similar

Tips

I have added dried lavender to the pillow by sprinkling it on the polyester filling. However, if the lavender was in a fabric sachet and then added to the pillow it could be removed and refreshed as needed.

Any other dried herbs could be substituted for the lavender, as desired.

SCENTED SLEEP PILLOW

Size: 7½in (18cm) square

PREPARATION

The pillow is made up of nine patchwork squares with appliquéd hearts on four of the squares. The pillow has a plain back and is filled with polyester toy stuffing and dried lavender.

CUTTING

All cutting instructions include a ¼in (0.65cm) seam allowance.

Peach fabric
- One 8in (20.3cm) square
- Four 3in (7.5cm) squares

Pink fabric
- Five 3in (7.5cm) squares
- Four heart motifs (see page 139)

METHOD

To stitch the appliqué:

1 Lay out the nine 3in (7.5cm) squares in the pattern shown in the photograph and stitch together into three rows of three squares. Press seams in the top and bottom row one way and those in the middle row in the opposite direction. Stitch the rows together. Press seams downwards. Appliqué a heart to each of the peach squares. This project has been appliquéd using zigzag stitch machine appliqué (see page 14).

To stitch the scented sleep pillow together:

2 With right sides together, place the unit completed in Step 1 on top of the 8in (20.3cm) peach square. Stitch around each side, leaving a 2in (5cm) gap in the middle of one side. Trim corners.

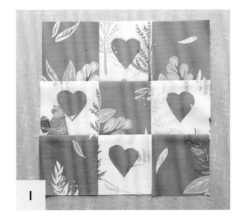

To finish the scented sleep pillow:

3 Turn the pillow through the gap so that it is right side out and press. Stuff lightly with the polyester toy filling. Add the dried lavender.

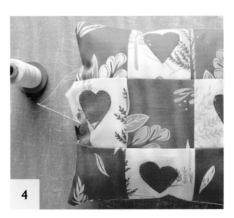

4 Close the opening with small, neat slip stitches.

HOT WATER BOTTLE COVER

There is nothing nicer on a cold evening than to snuggle up with a hot water bottle. This stylish cover is softly padded, which makes it super comforting, and it will fit most hot water bottles. It makes the perfect gift for anyone who feels the cold!

SKILL LEVEL: EASY

YOU'LL NEED

FABRIC
Requirements based on fabrics with a useable width of 42in (107cm):

- 12in (30cm) peach floral for the outer cover and appliqué

- 20in (50cm) beige patterned for the outer cover and lining

WADDING (BATTING)
- 12in (30cm) fusible wadding (batting)

HABERDASHERY
- Neutral thread for piecing

- Peach thread for quilting

- 40in (1m) beige ribbon, 1in (2.5cm) wide

Tips

The cover fits a hot water bottle measuring 8 × 13in (20.3 × 33cm); however, there is room within the cover for a slightly larger or smaller hot water bottle.

After sewing the ribbon to the outer section, fold it up and into the fabric before stitching the outer units together. This will ensure that the ribbon does not get caught in the stitching.

HOT WATER BOTTLE COVER

Size: 10 x 15in (25 x 38cm)

PREPARATION

The hot water bottle cover features two fabrics on each outer side with appliquéd hearts on the front. The cover is finished with a ribbon tie.

CUTTING

All cutting instructions include a ¼in (0.65cm) seam allowance.

Peach floral fabric
- Two 10½ x 8¾in (26.5 x 22.2cm) rectangles
- Three heart motifs (see page 139)

Beige patterned fabric
- Two 10½ x 7¼in (26.5 x 18.4cm) rectangles
- Two 15½ x 10½in (39.4 x 26.5cm) rectangles

Fusible wadding (batting)
- Two 15½ x 10½in (39.4 x 26.5cm) rectangles

METHOD

To stitch the appliqué:

1 Take one 10½ × 7¼in (26.5 × 18.4cm) beige patterned rectangle and appliqué three hearts to the fabric, positioning them in a random arrangement across the centre of the rectangle. This project has been appliquéd using blanket stitch hand appliqué (see page 16).

To stitch the hot water bottle cover together:

2 Stitch each 10½ × 7¼in (26.5 × 18.4cm) beige patterned rectangle to a 10½ × 8¾in (26.5 × 22.2cm) peach floral rectangle. Press seams towards the peach floral rectangles.

3 Iron the fusible wadding (batting) to the wrong side of each of the units completed in Step 2.

4 Using peach thread, quilt vertical lines from top to bottom through both the fabric and the wadding (batting) at 2in (5cm) intervals.

5 Fold the ribbon in half and place it on the right side of the back of the cover, in the centre, 3¼in (8.2cm) down from the top raw edge. Pin in place in the centre and stitch down with one vertical line of stitching. Place the two quilted units right sides together and stitch up each long side and across the bottom. Trim corners and turn through.

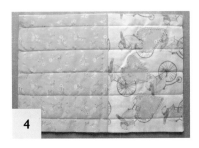

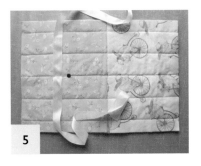

6 To stitch the lining, place the two 15½ x 10½in (39.4 x 26.5cm) beige patterned rectangles right sides together. Pin and stitch up each long side and across the bottom, leaving a 4in (10cm) gap in stitching in the middle of one side. Trim corners.

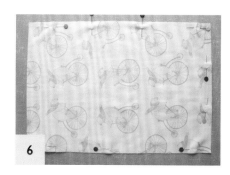

7 Place the outer hot water bottle cover inside the lining, right sides together, and pin all the way around the top edge. Sew around the edge, matching the side seams. Turn the hot water bottle cover right side out through the opening in the lining and stitch the opening closed with small neat slip stitches.

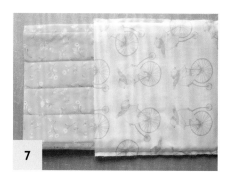

To finish the hot water bottle cover:

8 Carefully press the top of the hot water bottle cover so that ¼in (0.65cm) of the lining is showing on the outside and pin in place. Stitch through the layers in the seam line around the top.

9 Place the hot water bottle inside the cover and tie the ribbon with a neat bow.

PYJAMA BAG

This handy pyjama bag is fully lined and decorated with cute clothing motifs. It is just the right size for nightwear of any shape or size and is perfect to pack in an overnight bag. The drawstring allows the bag to be hung neatly out of the way when not in use.

SKILL LEVEL: REQUIRES EXPERIENCE

YOU'LL NEED

FABRIC

Requirements based on fabrics with a useable width of 42in (107cm):

- 20in (50cm) blue for the outer bag and drawstrings

- 30in (76cm) cream pattern for the outer bag and lining

- Fabric scraps in burgundy for the appliqué

HABERDASHERY

- Neutral thread for piecing

- Pale blue thread for topstitching

- Large safety pin for threading

> **Tip**
>
> This pyjama bag pattern could be doubled up as a sports kit or laundry bag, so it really has a variety of purposes. Just adapt the fabric choices appropriately.

PYJAMA BAG

Size: 20 × 12in (50 × 30cm)

PREPARATION

Both outer sides of the pyjama bag have the same fabric strips, while the front of the bag features appliquéd clothing. The drawstring ties sit in a casing across the top of the bag.

CUTTING

All cutting instructions include a ¼in (0.65cm) seam allowance.

Blue fabric
- Two 12½ × 8½in (31.7 × 21.6cm) rectangles
- Four 12½ × 4½in (31.7 × 11.5cm) rectangles
- Two 1½ × 40in (4 × 101.6cm) strips

Cream fabric
- Four 12½ × 2½in (31.7 × 6.3cm) strips
- Two 20 × 12½in (50 × 31.7cm) rectangles

Burgundy fabric scraps
- Two jumper and two trouser motifs (see page 140)

METHOD

To stitch the appliqué:

1 Take one 12½ × 4½in (31.7 × 11.5cm) blue rectangle and appliqué two jumper and two trouser motifs along the centre of the fabric. Position the motifs so that they are 1in (2.5cm) away from any raw edge. This project has been appliquéd using zigzag stitch machine appliqué (see page 14).

To stitch the pyjama bag together:

2 To stitch the front of the outer bag, take the unit completed in Step 1 and stitch a 12½ × 2½in (31.7 × 6.3cm) cream strip to each side. Press seams towards the blue rectangle. Stitch a 12½ × 8½in (31.7 × 21.6cm) blue rectangle to the top of this unit and a 12½ × 4½in (31.7 × 11.5cm) blue rectangle to the bottom. Press seams towards the blue rectangles. Repeat with the remaining fabrics for the back of the outer bag.

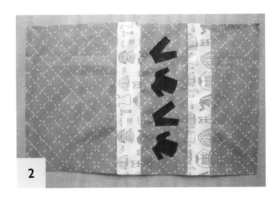

3 On both of the long sides of each of the outer bag panels completed in Step 2, measure and mark 2in (5cm) and 3in (7.5cm) from the top on the outer edge. Place the outer bag panels right sides together and pin each side and across the bottom, matching the seams. Do not pin between the 2in (5cm) and 3in (7.5cm) markings. Stitch down each side, stopping the stitching between the markings and stitch across the bottom of the bag. Press seams open and clip corners. Turn through.

4 To stitch the lining, take the two 20 × 12½in (50 × 31.7cm) cream rectangles. Pin them right sides together and stitch down each side and across the bottom, leaving a 5in (12.7cm) gap for turning in the bottom. Trim corners.

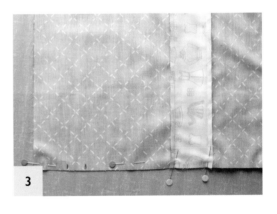

5 Place the outer bag inside the lining, right sides together, and pin all the way around the top edge. Sew around the edge, matching the side seams. Turn the bag through the gap in the lining. Push out the corners and stitch the gap closed with small, neat slip stitches.

6 Press and topstitch with the pale blue thread around the top edge, ⅛in (0.32cm) away from the top of the bag.

To finish the pyjama bag:

7 To stitch the casing for the drawstrings, measure 1¾in (4.4cm) down from the top of the bag and draw a line horizontally across the bag on both sides using a marking pencil. Draw another line 1in (2.5cm) away from this line. The lines should align with the 1in (2.5cm) gaps left in the bag seams. Stitch along both of these drawn lines using the pale blue thread.

8 To stitch the drawstrings, take the two 1½ × 40in (4 × 101.6cm) blue strips and press under ¼in (0.65cm) along each long side. Fold the strips of fabric wrong sides together so that the folded edges meet. Stitch ⅛in (0.32cm) away from the folded edge.

9 To insert the drawstrings in the casing, attach the safety pin to one end of one of the drawstring ties. Starting on the right-hand side, thread the end of the drawstring with the safety pin through the front casing, back through the back casing and tie the ends in a knot on the right side. Repeat the process with the second drawstring, but this time start on the left-hand side.

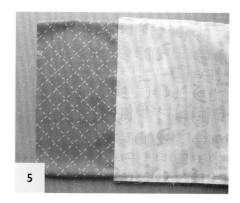

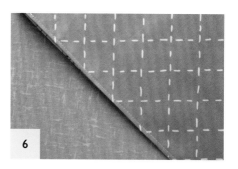

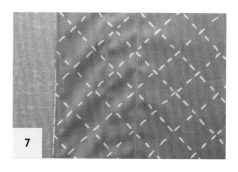

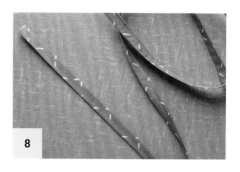

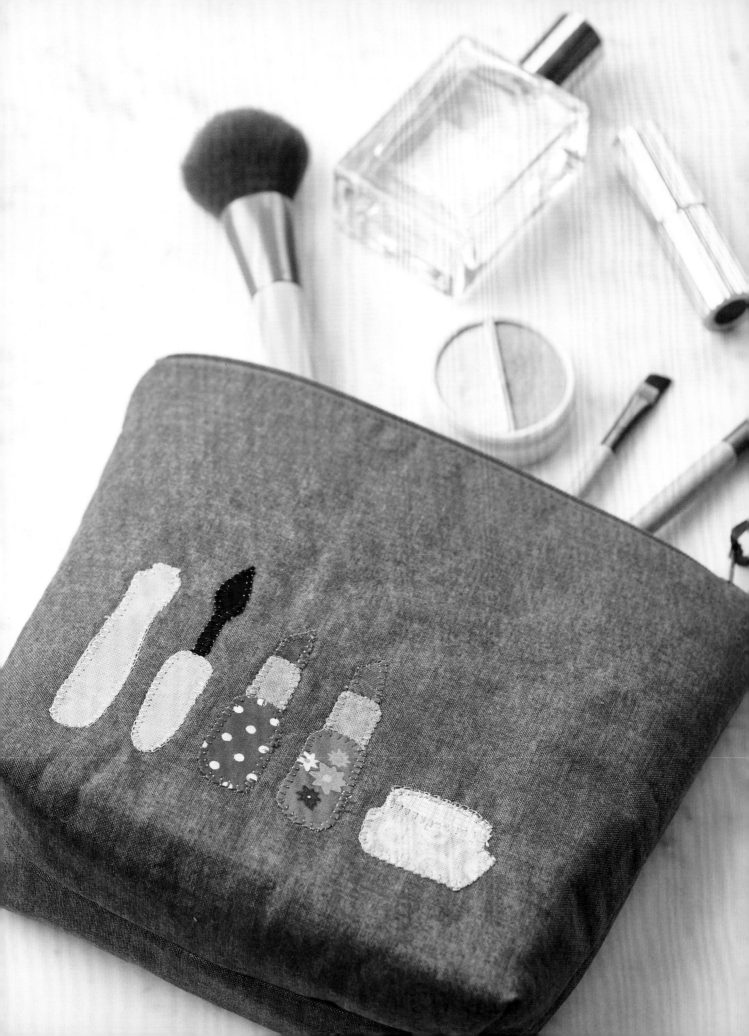

MAKE-UP BAG

Treat yourself with this fashionable but functional zipped make-up bag, perfect for storing those essential beauty items. Slip it into your handbag or suitcase to ensure you look your best every day. This would also make a lovely birthday present for a fashion-conscious teenager or a thoughtful gift to take to a pamper party.

SKILL LEVEL: REQUIRES EXPERIENCE

YOU'LL NEED

FABRIC

Requirements based on fabrics with a useable width of 42in (107cm):

- 10in (25cm) blue for the outer pouch

- 10in (25cm) floral for the lining

- Fabric scraps in yellow, black, red, pink, orange, red spot, pink floral, light pink and beige for the appliqué

WADDING (BATTING)

- 10in (25cm) fusible wadding (batting)

HABERDASHERY

- Neutral thread for piecing

- Blue thread for topstitching

- One 8in (20.3cm) blue zip

- 4in (10cm) pink ribbon, ⅛in (0.32cm) wide

Tips

It's really important to open the zip halfway in Step 5. If you forget, then you will be unable to turn the make-up bag out to the right side.

When stitching the outer sections and lining panels together it makes a difference if the teeth of the zip point towards the lining fabric. This makes the part of the pouch where the zip meets the side seams look much neater.

MAKE-UP BAG

. . . .

Size: 8½ × 7 × 2½in (21.6 × 17.8 × 6.3cm)

PREPARATION

. . . .

The make-up bag has a plain outer with
appliquéd make-up motifs and a floral lining.
It is softly padded with wadding (batting)
and finished with a ribbon pull on the zip.

CUTTING

. . . .

All cutting instructions include
a ¼in (0.65cm) seam allowance.

Blue fabric
• Two 9 × 8½in (23 × 21.6cm) rectangles

Floral fabric
• Two 9 × 8¼in (23 × 21cm) rectangles

Fabric scraps
• One mascara tube and wand,
  two lipsticks and one face cream pot
  motifs (see page 140)

Fusible wadding (batting)
• Two 9 × 8½in (23 × 21.6cm) rectangles

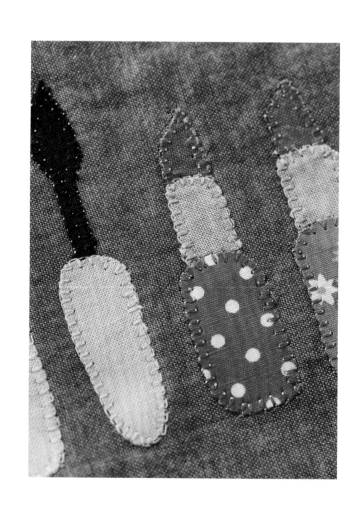

METHOD

. . . .

To stitch the appliqué:

1 Take one 9 × 8½in (23 × 21.6cm) blue rectangle and appliqué one mascara tube, one mascara wand, two lipsticks and one face cream pot motif to the fabric. Position the motifs so that they are 2½in (6.3cm) away from the bottom 9in (23cm) raw edge and 2in (5cm) away from the sides. This project has been appliquéd using blanket stitch machine appliqué (see page 15).

To stitch the make-up bag together:

2 Iron the fusible wadding (batting) to the wrong side of each blue rectangle.

To attach the zip:

3 Place the first outer pouch section right side up and place the zip face down on front of it, matching the top edge. Pin in place and then pin the 9 × 8¼in (23 × 21cm) floral rectangle on top, right side down. Stitch along the top edge to secure the lining, zip and outer pouch. Repeat to attach the zip to the second pouch section.

4 Open out each panel and press. Stitch ⅛in (0.32cm) each side of the zip with the blue thread.

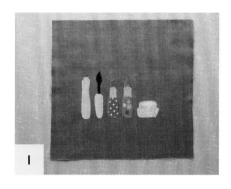

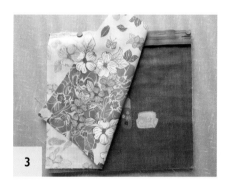

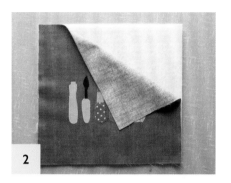

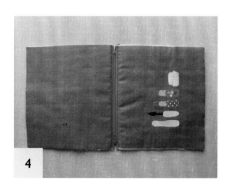

To finish the make-up bag:

5 Open the zip halfway and place the two outer pouch sections right sides together, and also the lining panels right sides together. Pin and stitch all the way around the edge, leaving a 3in (7.5cm) gap in stitching in the bottom of the lining.

6 To shape the base, match the centre fold of the base with the side seam. Measure 1¼in (3.1cm) along the seam line and stitch across. Cut off the excess fabric. Repeat on the other corner, and then on both corners of the lining.

7 Turn the pouch through the opening in the lining so it is right side out. Stitch the opening closed with neat slip stitches. Press well. To finish, tie the ribbon to the zip pull.

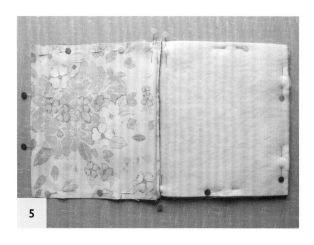

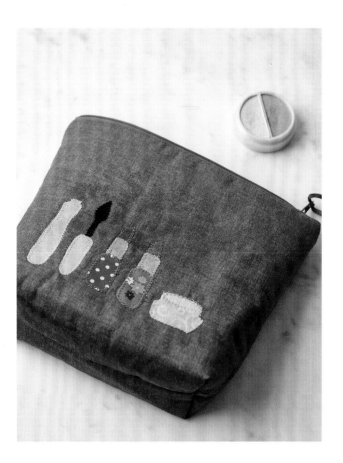

COIN PURSE

This cute coin purse is robust enough for everyday use and can be made in a variety of fabrics to match your glasses case or shopping bags. It is quick enough to stitch up in an hour or so, makes a great gift and is ideal for using up small fabric scraps.

SKILL LEVEL: EASY

YOU'LL NEED

FABRIC

Requirements based on fabrics with a useable width of 42in (107cm):

- 6in (15.2cm) pink for the outer purse and flap

- 6in (15.2cm) pale green for the lining and flap lining

- Fabric scraps in jade and pink for the motifs

HABERDASHERY

- 6in (15.2cm) fusible medium-weight interfacing

- Neutral thread for piecing

- Pink thread for topstitching

- One ½in (1.3cm) diameter magnetic snap

Tips

In Step 8, when you are stitching the outer purse section together, push the flap section right down inside the purse and make sure that you do not catch the flap in the side seams.

If you do not wish to use a magnetic snap you could substitute it with a button and button hole.

COIN PURSE

Size: 4½ × 4in (11.5 × 10cm)

PREPARATION

The purse uses one fabric for the outer and the second fabric for the lining. The flap is appliquéd with two small flower motifs. The outer sections are strengthened with interfacing, which helps the purse to keep its shape, and it is finished with a small magnetic snap.

CUTTING

All cutting instructions include a ¼in (0.65cm) seam allowance.

Pink fabric
- One 8 × 5in (20.3 × 12.7cm) rectangle
- One 5 × 3½in (12.7 × 8.9cm) rectangle

Pale green fabric
- One 8 × 5in (20.3 × 12.7cm) rectangle
- One 5 × 3½in (12.7 × 8.9cm) rectangle

Fabric scraps
- Two flower motifs (see page 139)

Fusible medium-weight interfacing
- One 8 × 5in (20.3 × 12.7cm) rectangle
- One 5 × 3½in (12.7 × 8.9cm) rectangle
- Two 1in (2.5cm) squares

METHOD

To shape the flap:

1 Take the 5 × 3½in (12.7 × 8.9cm) pink, pale green and fusible interfacing rectangles, measure in 1in (2.5cm) from each corner along one 5in (12.7cm) edge and mark with a marking pencil. Repeat on each opposite corner. Draw a line from the unmarked corner on the same side to the mark. Cut on the drawn line. Repeat on the opposite side.

To stitch the appliqué:

2 On the 5 × 3½in (12.7 × 8.9cm) pink fabric from Step 1, appliqué two flower motifs, ensuring that the motifs are positioned ½in (1.3cm) away from any outer edge. This project has been stitched using blanket stitch machine appliqué (see page 15).

To stitch the coin purse together:

3 To stitch the flap, iron the fusible interfacing to the wrong side of the unit completed in Step 2. To insert one side of the magnetic snap, take the 5 × 3½in (12.7 × 8.9cm) pale green fabric, measure ¾in (1.9cm) down from the centre of the outer shaped edge and mark the point with a dot. Iron a 1in (2.5cm) square of interfacing to the wrong side of the lining over the marked dot. Make two small holes for the prongs of the magnetic snap. Inset the prongs through the holes on the right side of the fabric, add the back plate and open the prongs so they lie flat.

4 Place the outer and lining flap units completed in Step 3 with right sides together, pin and stitch around three sides, leaving the 5in (12.7cm) side open.

5 Clip corners and turn through. Press well and topstitch around the three folded edges with the pink thread, ⅛in (0.32cm) in from the outer edge.

6 To stitch the second part of the snap to the main body of the purse, take the 8 × 5in (20.3 × 12.7cm) pink rectangle and mark a point with a dot 2¾in (7cm) in the centre from one of the 5in (12.7cm) edges. Iron a 1in (2.5cm) square of interfacing to the wrong side of the fabric over the marked dot. Insert the snap following the instructions in Step 3. Iron the 8 × 5in (20.3 × 12.7cm) interfacing rectangle to the wrong side of this unit.

7 Take the completed flap unit and the outer purse unit completed in Step 6 and, with right sides together, stitch the raw edge of the flap to the raw edge of the outer section. The snap on the main purse unit will be at the opposite end to the flap. Stitch with a ⅛in (0.32cm) seam.

8 With right sides together, fold up the outer section so that the short ends match, and stitch down each side. Trim corners. Repeat with the 8 × 5in (20.3 × 12.7cm) pale green rectangle, but leave a 1½in (4cm) gap in the stitching in the middle of one side.

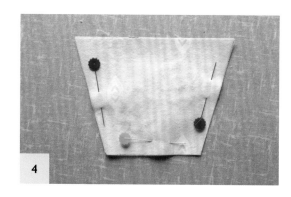

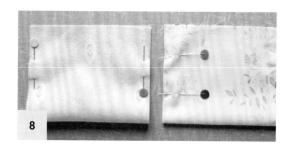

To finish the coin purse:

9 Turn the outer purse right side out. Place the outer purse inside the lining so that the right side of the lining is facing the right side of the purse. Match the side seams and pin to hold in place. Stitch around the top. Turn the purse through the opening in the lining and stitch the gap in the lining closed with small, neat slip stitches. Give the coin purse a final press to finish.

GLASSES CASE

This cute glasses case is ideal for your sunglasses or reading glasses and will slip easily into your handbag. The padded fabric will protect your eyewear when you are out and about. Stitch your case in a bright fabric and you'll be sure to never lose those glasses again!

SKILL LEVEL: REQUIRES EXPERIENCE

YOU'LL NEED

FABRIC
Requirements based on fabrics with a useable width of 42in (107cm):

- 6in (15.2cm) jade for the outer case

- 6in (15.2cm) pale green for the lining

- 12in (30cm) square pink for the bias binding

- Fabric scrap in pink for the motif

WADDING (BATTING)
- 6in (15.2cm) fusible wadding (batting)

HABERDASHERY
- Neutral thread for piecing

- 1in (2.5cm) square of hook and loop sew-on tape

Tips

Although this case fits a standard-size pair of glasses, different styles of glasses vary in shape and size, so the pattern may need adjusting to fit. When measuring your glasses, remember to allow for wadding (batting). Bear in mind the bias binding also reduces the dimension of the glasses case once stitched in place.

The glasses case could be made in the same fabric as the coin purse (see page 96) for a matching set.

GLASSES CASE

Size: 7 x 4in (17.8 x 10cm)

PREPARATION

The glasses case is fully lined and padded and features an appliquéd glasses motif on the front. The outer edges are finished with bias binding and a hook and loop fastening.

CUTTING

All cutting instructions include a ¼in (0.65cm) seam allowance.

Jade fabric
- One 9¾ x 4in (24.7 x 10cm) rectangle
- One 6 x 4in (15.2 x 10cm) rectangle

Pale green fabric
- One 9¾ x 4in (24.7 x 10cm) rectangle
- One 6 x 4in (15.2 x 10cm) rectangle

Pink fabric
- One 1 x 32in (2.5 x 81.3cm) pink bias strip (join to get the required length)
- One glasses motif (see page 140)

Fusible wadding (batting)
- One 9¾ x 4in (24.7 x 10cm) rectangle
- One 6 x 4in (15.2 x 10cm) rectangle

METHOD

To stitch the appliqué:

1 On the 6 x 4in (15.2 x 10cm) jade rectangle, appliqué the glasses motif on the diagonal, 1½in (4cm) from the bottom edge. This project has been stitched using blanket stitch machine appliqué (see page 15).

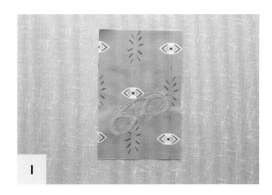

To stitch the glasses case together:

2 To curve the top folded section of the glasses case, take the 9¾ x 4in (24.7 x 10cm) jade, green and fusible wadding rectangles and, using a cup or circle template with a diameter of 2in (5cm), draw a curved edge on each top corner. Cut along the curve.

3 To curve the bottom of the glasses case, take the units from Step 2 and the 6 x 4in (15.2 x 10cm) jade, green and fusible wadding rectangles. Measure ½in (1.3cm) up from each lower corner and across the bottom and mark the points. Cut a small curve between these points on both bottom corners.

4 Stitch the hook side of the hook and loop tape to the 9¾ x 4in (24.7 x 10cm) green rectangle, positioning the tape in the centre, ½in (1.3cm) from the curved top of the rectangle. Stitch the loop side of the tape to the 6 x 4in (15.2 x 10cm) jade rectangle, positioning the tape in the centre, ½in (1.3cm) from the straight top edge of the rectangle.

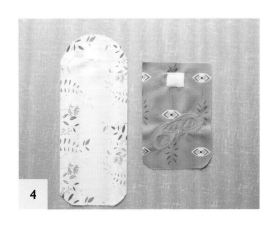

5 Iron the fusible wadding (batting) to the wrong side of both jade units and place these units on top of the corresponding lining fabrics so that the wrong sides of the fabric are facing each other. Pin in place.

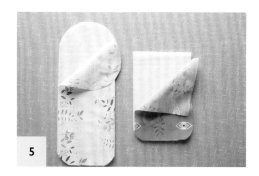

6 To make the bias binding, take the 1 × 32in (2.5 × 81.3cm) pink bias strip and fold and then iron under ¼in (0.65cm) on one long edge.

7 Take the 6 × 4in (15.2 × 10cm) unit completed in Step 5 and place the raw edge of the bias binding right side facing the 4in (10cm) straight edge and, matching the raw edges, stitch to the unit. Cut the binding strip level with the outer edge. Fold the binding over the outer edge to the lining side and slip stitch in place.

To finish the glasses case:

8 Place the 6 × 4in (15.2 × 10cm) unit on top of the 9¾ × 4in (24.7 × 10cm) unit so that the curved bottom matches. Pin in place. Using a ⅛in (0.32cm) seam, stitch through all layers, securing the two units together.

9 To attach the bias binding to the outer edge of the glasses case, turn under one short end and place the raw edge of the binding right side facing the case, matching the raw edges. Stitch around the outer edge. When you get to the place where you started, overlap the binding by ¼in (0.65cm) to hide the raw edge. Clip the curves. Fold the binding over the outer edge of the case and slipstitch in place. Give the glasses case a final press.

GIFT TAGS

Tie a handmade tag to a present or bouquet of flowers for personalized gift giving. These gift tags are a speedy one-hour project, and could be made in batches so that you always have some to hand. The sweet little house motif would make them the perfect finishing touch for that special house-warming gift.

SKILL LEVEL: EASY

YOU'LL NEED

FABRIC

Requirements based on fabrics with a useable width of 42in (107cm):

- 4in (10cm) yellow for the background

- 4in (10cm) purple for the background

- 5in (12.7cm) grey felt for the base

- 5in (12.7cm) cream felt for the base

- Fabric scraps in blue, red, stripe, yellow, navy and orange for the appliqué

HABERDASHERY

- Neutral thread for piecing

- Black embroidery thread

- 12in (30.5cm) red ribbon, ¼in (0.65cm) wide

- 12in (30.5cm) purple ribbon, ¼in (0.65cm) wide

Tips

If you wish to include a message on your gift tag, iron a piece of fusible interfacing to the back of the tag on the felt base. You can then write on the interfacing.

Gift tags can be personalized with other appliquéd motifs to suit the recipient or occasion.

GIFT TAGS

Size: 4½ x 3½in (11.5 x 8.9cm)

PREPARATION

The fabric requirements allow for two gift tags. Each gift tag has an appliquéd house stitched to a fabric background, which is then mounted on a felt base.

CUTTING

All cutting instructions include a ¼in (0.65cm) seam allowance.

Yellow fabric
• One 4 x 3in (10 x 7.5cm) rectangle

Purple fabric
• One 4 x 3in (10 x 7.5cm) rectangle

Grey felt
• One 4½ x 3½in (11.5 x 8.9cm) rectangle

Cream felt
• One 4½ x 3½in (11.5 x 8.9cm) rectangle

Fabric scraps
• Two house motifs (see page 141)

METHOD
(TO MAKE ONE GIFT TAG)

To stitch the appliqué:

1 Take the 4 x 3in (10 x 7.5cm) yellow rectangle and appliqué one house motif to the fabric, positioning it in the centre. This project has been appliquéd using needle turn hand appliqué (see page 15). Using the black embroidery thread, stitch a French knot to the door to make a doorknob.

To stitch the gift tag together:

2 Pull the threads from the outer edges of the yellow fabric so that a ¼in (0.65cm) frayed edge appears on all four sides of the yellow rectangle.

3 Take the red ribbon and fold in half. Slip the folded edge in between the appliquéd yellow rectangle and the 4½ x 3½in (11.5 x 8.9cm) grey felt rectangle, placing it in the centre at the top so that ¼in (0.65cm) of the ribbon is tucked inside. Pin the fabric and the felt together on all four sides.

To finish the gift tag:

4 Stitch around the unit pinned together in Step 3, as close as possible to the frayed edge, to secure the layers together.

GIFT BAGS

There is nothing nicer than giving a gift in a handmade bag. These drawstring gift bags, embellished with a charming flowerpot motif, are quick and easy to stitch and just the right size for any number of little gifts. Alternatively, they would be ideal for wedding favours or party bags.

SKILL LEVEL: EASY

YOU'LL NEED

FABRIC
Requirements based on fabrics with a useable width of 42in (107cm):

- 10in (25cm) white for the outer bag

- 10in (25cm) pale green for the outer bag

- Fabric scraps in gold, purple and turquoise for the appliqué

HABERDASHERY
- Neutral thread for piecing

- Green embroidery thread

- One purple button and one pink button

- 40in (1m) gold ribbon, ½in (1.3cm) wide

- 40in (1m) lilac ribbon, ½in (1.3cm) wide

- Small safety pin for threading

Tips

These gift bags could be personalized with appliquéd or embroidered names or motifs to suit the recipient.

Alternatively, the bags could be made in fabrics such as silk or taffeta to suit the occasion.

GIFT BAGS

Size: 8½ × 5½in (21.6 × 14cm)

PREPARATION

The fabric requirements allow for two gift bags. Each gift bag has a folded top with a casing for the ribbon drawstring and features and appliquéd flower motif.

CUTTING

All cutting instructions include a ¼in (0.65cm) seam allowance.

White fabric
•   Two 10 × 6in (25 × 15.2cm) rectangles

Pale green fabric
•   Two 10 × 6in (25 × 15.2cm) rectangles

Fabric scraps
•   Two flowerpots and flower motifs (see page 138)

METHOD
(TO MAKE ONE GIFT BAG)

To stitch the appliqué:

1 Take one 10 x 6in (25 x 15.2cm) white rectangle and appliqué one flowerpot and flower motif to the fabric, positioning the pot 1½in (4cm) up from the bottom 6in (15.2cm) raw edge. This project has been appliquéd using needle turn hand appliqué (see page 15). Using the green embroidery thread, stitch a line of backstitch between the pot and the flower. Stitch the pink button to the centre of the flower.

To stitch the gift bag together:

2 To make the drawstring casing, take the two 10 x 6in (25 x 15.2cm) white rectangles and fold over 1½in (4cm) on one 6in (15.2cm) edge of each so that the wrong sides are together. Press well and pin to hold in place. On each of these outer bag panels and on both long sides, measure and mark ½in (1.3cm) and 1in (2.5cm) from the top of the folded edge.

3 Place the outer bag panels right sides together and pin each side and across the bottom. Stitch down each side, stopping the stitching between the markings, and stitch across the bottom of the bag. Clip corners.

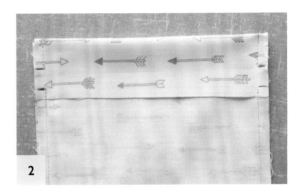

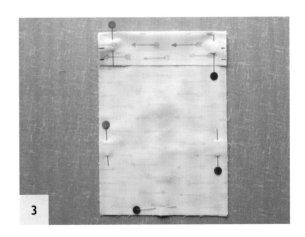

4 To stitch the drawstring casing, use a marking pencil to draw a horizontal line across the bag on both sides between the two ½in (1.3cm) markings. Repeat between the 1in (2.5cm) markings. These lines should align with the gaps left in the bag side seams. Stitch along both of these drawn lines. Turn the bag through.

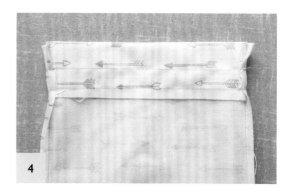

To finish the gift bag:

5 Cut the gold ribbon in half so that each piece measures 20in (50cm). Attach the safety pin to one end of one piece of ribbon. Starting on the right-hand side, thread the end of the ribbon with the safety pin through the front casing, back through the back casing and tie the ends with a knot on the right side. Remove the safety pin and repeat the process with the second piece of ribbon, this time starting on the left-hand side.

TULIP PICTURE

Create your own piece of wall art with this stylized appliquéd tulip, framed in an embroidery hoop. So easy to make, the bold colours and simple design are guaranteed to brighten up a plain wall in any room. Why not get creative and vary the colours or give some other flower shapes a try?

SKILL LEVEL: EASY

YOU'LL NEED

FABRIC

Requirements based on fabrics with a useable width of 42in (107cm):

- 16in (40.6cm) square of cream for the background

- Small fabric scraps in orange and green for the appliqué

- 11in (27.9cm) square of cream felt

HABERDASHERY

- One 10in (25cm) wooden hoop with an inner and outer frame

- Neutral thread for piecing

- Fabric glue

- 12in (30.5cm) orange ribbon, ⅛in (0.32cm) wide

Tips

This project could be adapted to fit hoops of different sizes by reducing or enlarging the tulip motif.

A set of pictures in three hoops of differing sizes would look very effective.

TULIP PICTURE

Size: 10in (25cm) diameter

PREPARATION

The picture in a hoop is made up of an appliquéd single tulip. The cream fabric is stretched around the hoop inner, trimmed and gathered on the back, and neatened to finish with a covering of felt.

CUTTING

All cutting instructions include a ¼in (0.65cm) seam allowance.

Cream fabric
- One 16in (40.6cm) square

Fabric scraps
- One tulip motif (see page 141)

Cream felt
- One 11in (27.9cm) square

METHOD

To stitch the appliqué:

1 Using a marking pencil, draw around the inner hoop frame onto the centre of the right side of the 16in (40.6cm) cream fabric square.

2 Appliqué the tulip onto the centre of the circle drawn in Step 1. This project has been appliquéd using straight stitch machine appliqué (see page 13).

To stitch the picture together:

3 Put the appliqué completed in Step 2 onto the inner hoop frame. Place the outer frame on top, ensuring that the tulip is centred in the middle of the frame and the frame screw is at the top. Tighten the screw and stretch the fabric so that it is taut. Turn the hoop over so that the wrong side is facing you and trim the excess fabric so that 2in (5cm) remains all the way around.

4 By hand, stitch a gathering thread all the way around the excess fabric, ¼in (0.65cm) in from the outer edge. Pull the thread up tightly and secure.

To finish the tulip picture:

5 Using a marking pencil, draw around the outer frame onto the 11in (27.9cm) square of cream felt. Cut the felt out carefully just inside the drawn line. Glue the felt circle to the reverse of the hoop, covering the gathered fabric.

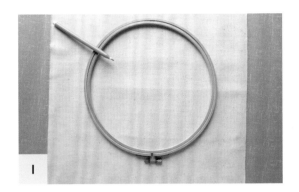

NOTICEBOARD

Use this fresh and summery plant-inspired noticeboard to help with day-to-day organization. The ribbon grid is great for tucking in letters and shopping lists to ensure that nothing is forgotten. The cork tile backing also enables you to pin your notes in place for extra security.

SKILL LEVEL: EASY

YOU'LL NEED

FABRIC

Requirements based on fabrics with a useable width of 42in (107cm):

- 14in (35.8cm) yellow floral for the background

- Fabric scraps in green and terracotta for the appliqué

HABERDASHERY

- 120in (3m) yellow ribbon, ½in (1.3cm) wide

- Yellow thread for piecing

- One 12in (30.5cm) square cork tile

- Fabric clips (optional)

- Wall stapler and/or strong parcel tape

Tips

I used a sewing machine to stitch the ribbon to the background fabric, but this entire project could be easily sewn by hand.

I used just four plant motifs, but additional motifs could be added to the outer squares, if desired.

NOTICEBOARD

Size: 12in (30.5cm) square

PREPARATION

The cork tile provides a stable base for the noticeboard, which is covered in fabric. Ribbon strips are stitched together at interconnecting points and secured to the back of the board.

CUTTING

All cutting instructions include a ¼in (0.65cm) seam allowance.

Yellow floral fabric
* One 14in (35.8cm) square

Fabric scraps
* Two round plant, two cacti and four plant pot motifs (see page 141)

METHOD

To mark up the noticeboard and stitch the appliqué:

1 Draw a line on the diagonal of the right side of the 14in (35.8cm) yellow floral fabric square from corner to corner. Draw a diagonal line 4in (10.2cm) on each side of this first line. Repeat on the other corner. On each of the four centrally marked diagonal squares appliqué a plant motif, ensuring that each plant is placed in the centre of each square. This project has been appliquéd using blanket stitch hand appliqué (see page 16).

To stitch the noticeboard together:

2 Lay the ribbon on the diagonally drawn centre line on the yellow floral square, ensuring that each end of the ribbon extends to the outer edge of the fabric square. Cut the ribbon to fit. Repeat with two further pieces of ribbon on the lines to each side of this first line. Pin the ribbon to the yellow fabric at each drawn intersection. Stitch three or four stitches at these intersections to secure the ribbon to the fabric.

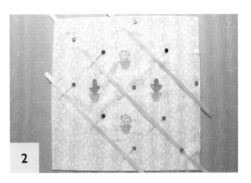

3 Repeat Step 2 with the remaining ribbon on the opposite diagonal lines but this time, where the ribbons intersect, stitch them to the fabric by making a small square of stitches through both layers of ribbon and the fabric.

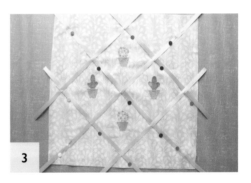

To finish the noticeboard:

4 Stretch the unit completed in Step 4 around the cork tile, ensuring that the appliqué and ribbons are centred on the tile. Hold in place with clips or pins.

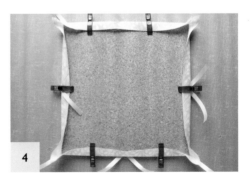

5 Staple the raw edges of the finished unit to the back of the tile and/or use parcel tape, as shown, to secure.

DOORSTOP

This lovely doorstop, decorated with a cute beach hut appliqué and weighted down with sand, is an essential but practical addition for any home. For a coordinating look, choose colours that match your interior or leftover fabrics from other furnishing projects.

SKILL LEVEL: EASY

YOU'LL NEED

FABRIC

Requirements based on fabrics with a useable width of 42in (107cm):

- 20in (50.8cm) blue star for the outer bag

- 10in (25cm) navy print for the lining top

- Fabric scraps in navy, navy print, red and yellow for the appliqué

HABERDASHERY

- Neutral thread for piecing

- 50in (127cm) string

- Plastic bag and sand for filling

Tips

If you do not wish to use sand as a filling for your doorstop, a brick can be used instead. Put the brick inside a plastic bag and wrap some wadding (batting) around the outside of the brick before inserting it in the doorstop.

String could be replaced with ribbon for a different look.

DOORSTOP

Size: 4 x 3 x 14in (10.2 x 7.5 x 35.8cm)

PREPARATION

The doorstop has a beach hut appliquéd motif on the front and a plain back. The gathered top of the doorstop is partly lined and tied up with string.

CUTTING

All cutting instructions include a ¼in (0.65cm) seam allowance.

Blue star fabric
• Two 18 x 8½in (45.7 x 21.6cm) rectangles

Navy print fabric
• Two 8½ x 8in (21.6 x 20.3cm) rectangles

Fabric scraps
• One beach hut motif (see page 141)

METHOD

To stitch the appliqué:

1 Appliqué the beach hut to the background fabric, positioning the bottom of the hut 4in (10.2cm) up from the bottom of the fabric. This project has been appliquéd using zigzag stitch machine appliqué (see page 14).

To stitch the project together:

2 Stitch an 8½ x 8in (21.6 x 20.3cm) navy rectangle to each 18 x 8½in (45.7 x 21.6cm) blue star rectangle. Press seams towards the navy fabric.

3 Fold the navy rectangle onto the blue rectangle so that the wrong sides are together and the seam line is at the top. Press. Topstitch ¼in (0.65cm) away from the seam line on both units.

4 Place both the units completed in Step 3 right sides together and stitch down each side and across the bottom. Neaten the seams with a zigzag stitch.

5 To shape the base, match the centre fold of the base with the side seam. Measure in 1½in (4cm) along the seam line, pin and stitch across. Cut off the excess fabric. Repeat on the other corner.

To finish the doorstop:

6 Turn the doorstop through and press carefully. Insert the plastic bag of sand into the doorstop so that it is two-thirds full. Fold the string in half and tie around the top of the doorstop.

LEAFY CUSHION

This grey and mustard cushion with its contemporary leaf design combines comfort with style, providing the perfect accent in a modern living room. Sew it in fabrics that complement your décor or choose contrasting colours to create a statement piece.

SKILL LEVEL: REQUIRES EXPERIENCE

YOU'LL NEED

FABRIC
Requirements based on fabrics with a useable width of 42in (107cm):

- 40in (1m) pale grey fabric for the cushion front and back

- 20in (50cm) cream fabric for the inner backing

- Fabric scraps in mustard and green for the appliqué

WADDING (BATTING)
- 18½in (47cm) square wadding (batting)

HABERDASHERY
- Neutral thread for piecing

- Grey thread for quilting

- 18in (45.7cm) square cushion pad

> **Tips**
>
> When quilting the vertical lines across the cushion, mark the centre line first and then stitch the lines from the centre. This helps to keep them straight.
>
> If you are short of time you could omit the quilting stage, leaving out the cream fabric or wadding (batting).

LEAFY CUSHION

Size: 18in (45.7cm) square

PREPARATION

The cushion centre is made up of a green stem with ten appliquéd mustard-coloured leaves. Five different mustard-coloured fabrics have been used for the leaves. The cover is quilted with vertical straight line quilting and finished with an envelope back.

CUTTING

All cutting instructions include a ¼in (0.65cm) seam allowance.

Grey fabric
*   One 18½in (47cm) square
*   Two 18½ x 14¼in (47 x 36.2cm) rectangles

Cream fabric
*   One 18½in (47cm) square

Fabric scraps
*   Two stem (see page 141) and ten leaf motifs (see page 138)

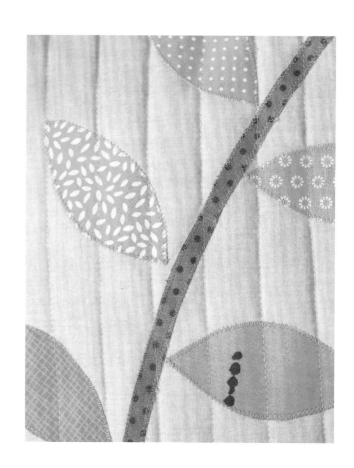

METHOD

To stitch the appliqué:

1 Take the 18½in (47cm) grey square and position the first stem 5in (12.7cm) in from the corner on the bottom edge of the fabric. Align the second stem motif with this first stem, overlapping the end by ¼in (0.65cm). Position five leaves on each side of the stem. Ensure that you stitch over the join on the stem. This project has been appliquéd using zigzag stitch machine appliqué (see page 14).

To stitch the cushion together:

2 Layer the cushion top by placing the 18½in (47cm) cream square wrong side up on a surface, followed by the wadding (batting) and then the cushion top, centrally and right side up. Secure with tacking (basting) stitches or quilters' pins placed at regular intervals.

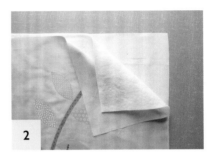

3 Using the grey thread, machine quilt vertical lines 1in (2.5cm) apart across the quilt top.

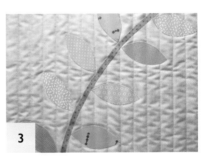

To finish the cushion:

4 To prepare the envelope back for the cushion, take the two 18½ × 14¼in (47 × 36.2cm) grey rectangles and on one 18½in (47cm) edge of each, fold and press ¼in (0.65cm) towards the wrong side. Fold the edge again, by 2in (5cm) to create a hem, press, then pin to hold in place.

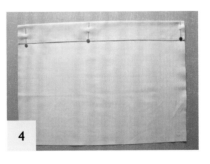

5 To stitch the cushion together, position one backing piece on the cushion front, right sides together with the folded edge in the middle, and pin around the outer edge. Repeat with the second backing piece. Stitch around the outer edge of the cushion. Trim corners and turn through so that the right side is facing out. Press well and insert the cushion pad.

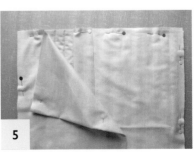

PEG BAG

This handy peg bag with its delightful clothing motifs is an essential item for washday. With its generous size, it will be roomy enough to store a mountain of pegs! The bag is fitted onto a coat hanger so it can be hung up on the washing line to keep all your pegs neat and tidy.

SKILL LEVEL: EASY

YOU'LL NEED

FABRIC

Requirements based on fabrics with a useable width of 42in (107cm):

- 20in (50cm) peach fabric for the front and back of the bag

- Fabric scraps in shades of blue for the appliqué

HABERDASHERY

- Neutral thread for piecing

- Black thread for stitching the washing line

- Black embroidery thread

- 20in (50cm) medium-weight fusible interfacing

- One child's coat hanger, 12in (30.5cm) wide

Tip

The instructions can be adjusted to make a peg bag to fit a different sized and shaped coat hanger. To do this, measure the width of the hanger and add 2in (5cm). This will give you the cutting measurement for the width. The length will remain the same. As you are using the coat hanger as a template to mark the slope of the hanger, this marking will be accurate every time.

PEG BAG

Size: 13½ × 14½in (34.2 × 37cm)

PREPARATION

The peg bag has the same fabric front and back and is lined with interfacing for added strength. Appliquéd clothing motifs are stitched to the front of the bag, which has an opening.

CUTTING

All cutting instructions include a ¼in (0.65cm) seam allowance.

Peach fabric
- One 15 × 14in (38.1 × 35.8cm) rectangle
- Two 14 × 8¼in (35.8 × 21cm) rectangles

Fabric scraps
- One shirt, one pair of trousers and two sock motifs (see page 140)

Fusible Interfacing
- One 15 × 14in (38.1 × 35.8cm) rectangle
- Two 14 × 8¼in (35.8 × 21cm) rectangles

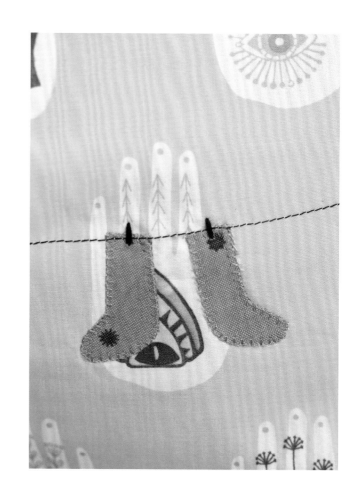

METHOD

To stitch the appliqué:

1 Take one 14 × 8¼in (35.8 × 21cm) peach rectangle and appliqué the clothing to the fabric, placing the motifs 2in (5cm) up from the bottom 14in (35.8cm) raw edge. Draw a washing line from one side to the other, touching the top of the motifs. Machine stitch over the line with black thread. To add pegs, use the black embroidery thread and add a small stitch onto each side of the motifs. This project has been appliquéd using blanket stitch machine appliqué (see page 15).

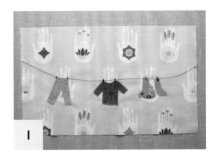

To stitch the peg bag together:

2 Iron the fusible interfacing rectangles to the corresponding peach rectangles.

3 Take the 15 × 14in (38.1 × 35.8cm) peach rectangle. Lay the hanger on top of the fabric as shown. Draw a line along each sloped edge of the top of the hanger, extending the drawn line to the outer edges .

4 Cut along the lines. Repeat on the remaining 14 × 8¼in (35.8 × 21cm) peach rectangle.

5 Take both 14 × 8¼in (35.8 × 21cm) peach rectangles and on the bottom of the shaped rectangle and top of the appliquéd rectangle, fold and press under ¼in (0.65cm). Stitch along the fold with a ⅛in (0.32cm) seam.

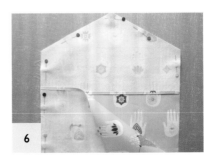

To finish the peg bag:

6 Position the top peg bag piece on the peg bag back, right sides together, with the folded edge in the middle. Pin around the outer edge. Repeat with the bottom peg bag front. Stitch around the outer edge, leaving a ½in (1.3cm) opening at the top point. Trim corners and turn through so that the right side is facing out. Press well and insert the coat hanger.

TEMPLATES

All templates are printed at 100% size. They have been reversed for transferring to the wrong side of the fabrics to be appliquéd.

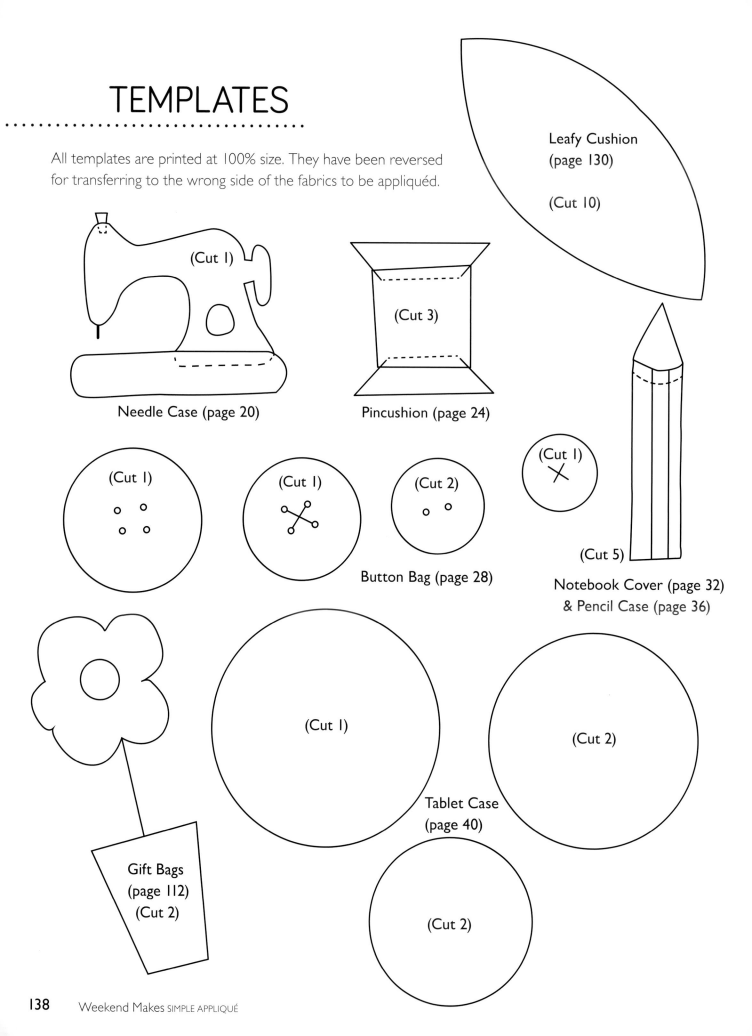

Leafy Cushion
(page 130)

(Cut 10)

(Cut 1)

Needle Case (page 20)

(Cut 3)

Pincushion (page 24)

(Cut 1)

(Cut 1)

(Cut 2)

Button Bag (page 28)

(Cut 1)

(Cut 5)

Notebook Cover (page 32)
& Pencil Case (page 36)

(Cut 1)

(Cut 2)

Tablet Case
(page 40)

(Cut 2)

Gift Bags
(page 112)
(Cut 2)

Coffee Cosy
(page 46)

(Cut 3)

Bread Basket
(page 54)

(Cut 1)

(Cut 2)

Egg Cosies (page 50)

Egg Cosies
(page 50)

Template For Cutting
(Cut 4)

Coasters
(page 70)

(Cut 2)

Scented Sleep
Pillow (page 74)
(Cut 4)

Hot Water
Bottle Cover
(page 78)

(Cut 3)

Coin Purse
(page 96)

(Cut 8)

(Cut 8)

(Cut 8)

Placemats
(page 60)

(Cut 2)

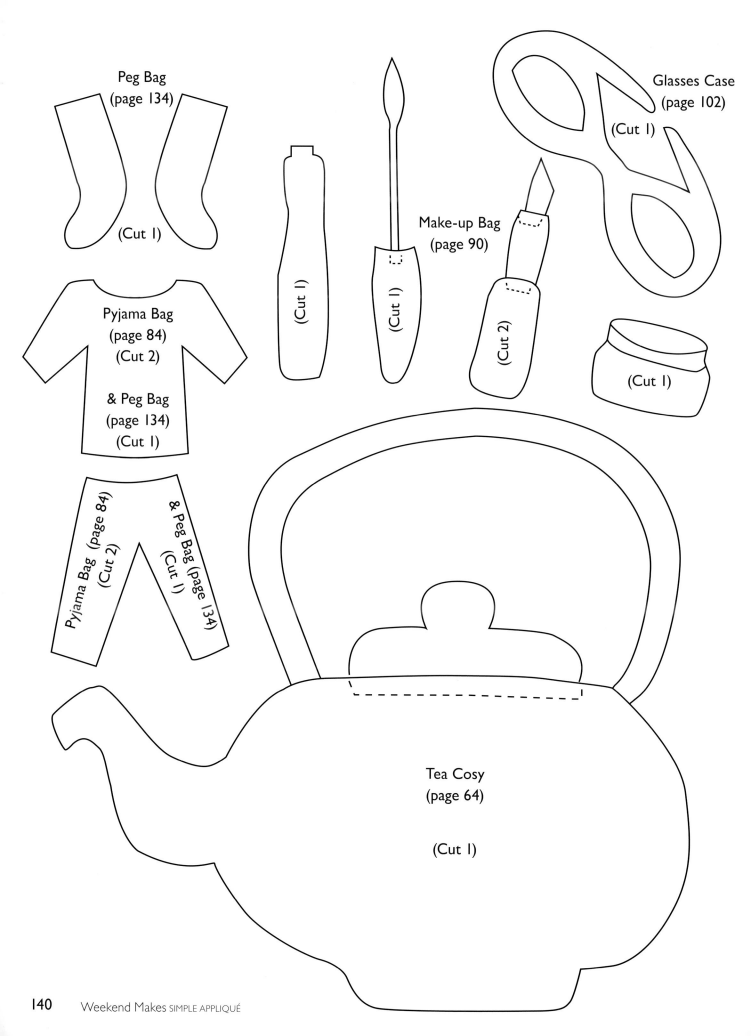

Peg Bag
(page 134)

(Cut 1)

Pyjama Bag
(page 84)
(Cut 2)

& Peg Bag
(page 134)
(Cut 1)

Pyjama Bag (page 84)
(Cut 2)

& Peg Bag (page 134)
(Cut 1)

(Cut 1)

(Cut 1)

Make-up Bag
(page 90)

(Cut 2)

Glasses Case
(page 102)

(Cut 1)

(Cut 1)

Tea Cosy
(page 64)

(Cut 1)

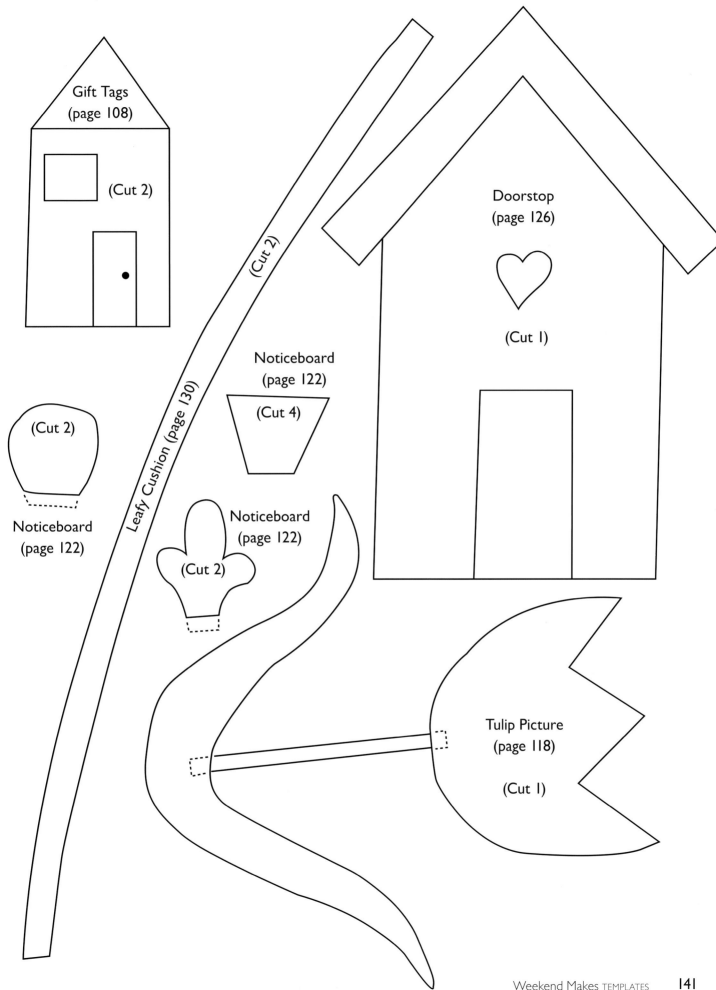

Gift Tags
(page 108)

(Cut 2)

Doorstop
(page 126)

(Cut 1)

Noticeboard
(page 122)

(Cut 4)

(Cut 2)

Noticeboard
(page 122)

Noticeboard
(page 122)

(Cut 2)

Leafy Cushion (page 130)

(Cut 2)

Tulip Picture
(page 118)

(Cut 1)

RESOURCES

Fabrics
Makower *www.makoweruk.com*
Hantex *www.hantex.co.uk*

Fusible wadding (batting)
Plush Addict *www.plushaddict.co.uk*

Wadding (batting)
Lady Sew and Sew
www.ladysewandsew.co.uk

Thread
Aurifil threads: *www.aurifil.com*

Interfacings
Vlieseline *www.vlieseline.com*

Fusible web and haberdashery
Just Between Friends
www.justbetweenfriends.co.uk

Sewing machine
Bernina *www.bernina.com*

ACKNOWLEDGEMENTS

I have so enjoyed designing, creating and writing the patterns for the projects in this book and am very grateful to everyone who played a part in the process. Many thanks to Darren and the team at Quail Studio for their hard work and great design. Thanks to Beth Dymond for her exacting technical editing. To Makower and Hantex, thank you for all the lovely fabrics to work with. Finally, thank you to my partner Alan, who is so supportive with my fabric obsession.

Janet Goddard

INDEX

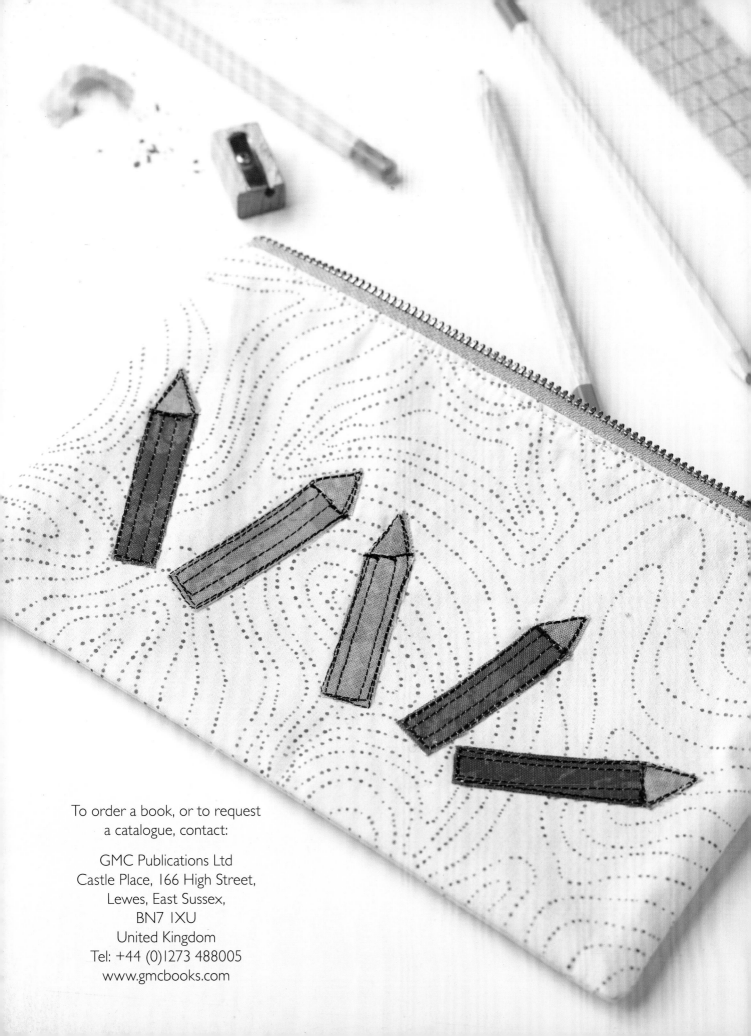

To order a book, or to request
a catalogue, contact:

GMC Publications Ltd
Castle Place, 166 High Street,
Lewes, East Sussex,
BN7 1XU
United Kingdom
Tel: +44 (0)1273 488005
www.gmcbooks.com